THE FAMILY CREATIVE WORK SHOP

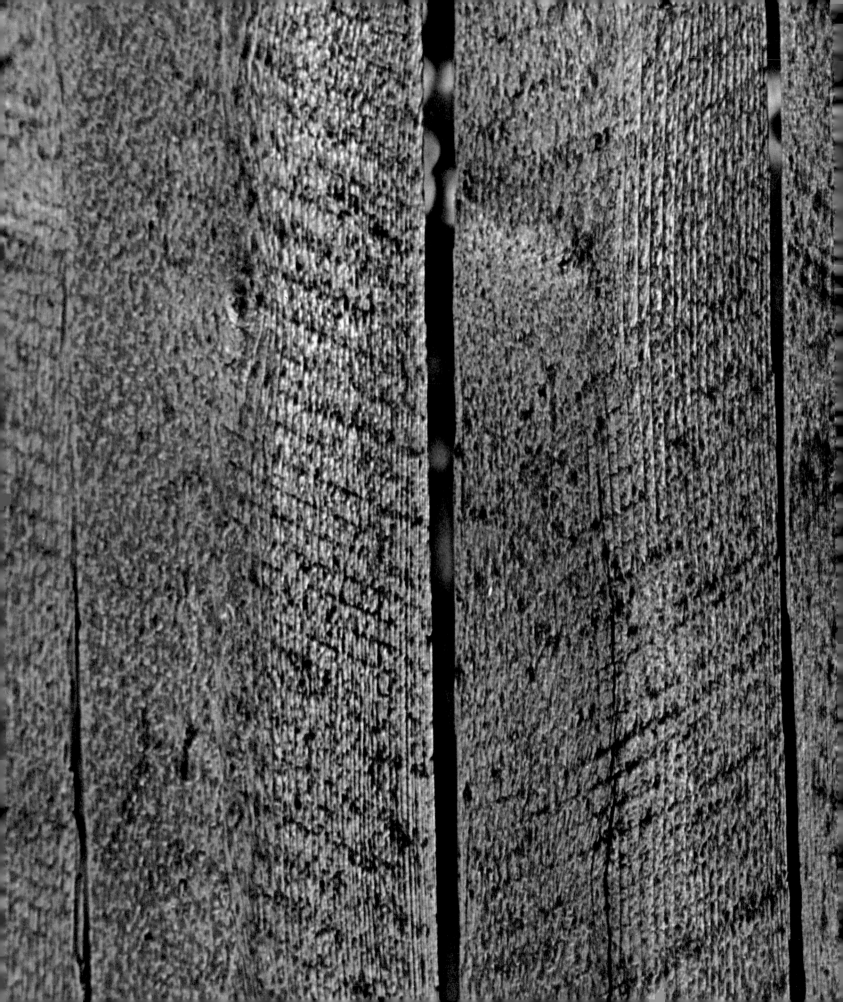

THE FAMILY CREATIVE WORKSHOP

23

Wire Sculpture, Wok Cookery
Wood Assemblages, Woven Tapestries
Wrapped and Coiled Work, Wycinanki
Yard Toys, Yarn Painting
Yo-Yos, Zoetrope Toys

Plenary Publications International, Inc.
New York and Amsterdam

Published by Plenary Publications International Incorporated 10 East 49th Street, N.Y., N.Y. 10017, for the Blue Mountain Crafts Council.

Library of Congress Catalog Card Number: 73-89331. Complete set International Standard Book Number: 0-88459-021-6. Volume 23 International Standard Book Number: 0-88459-023-2. Second Printing Manufactured in the United States of America. Printed and bound by the W.A. Krueger Company, Brookfield, Wisconsin.

Printing preparation by Lanman Lithoplate Comoany.

Publishers:
Plenary Publications International, Incorporated
10 East 49th Street
New York, N.Y. 10017

James Wagenvoord
EDITOR-IN-CHIEF

Jerry Curcio
PRODUCTION MANAGER

Jo Springer
VOLUME EDITOR

Joanne Delaney
Ellen Foley
EDITORIAL ASSISTANTS

Editorial preparation:
Tree Communications, Inc.
250 Park Avenue South
New York, New York 10003

Rodney Friedman
EDITORIAL DIRECTOR

Ronald Gross
DESIGN DIRECTOR

Paul Levin
DIRECTOR OF PHOTOGRAPHY

Donal Dinwiddie
CONSULTING EDITOR

Jill Munves
TEXT EDITOR

Sonja Douglas
ART DIRECTOR

Marsha Gold
DESIGNER

Lucille O'Brien
EDITORIAL PRODUCTION

Ruth Forst Michel
COPYREADER

Eva Gold
ADMINISTRATIVE MANAGER

Editors for this volume:
Andrea DiNoto
YARD TOYS

Michael Donner
WOOD ASSEMBLAGES
WYCINANKI

Linda Hetzer
WIRE SCULPTURE
WRAPPED AND COILED WORK

Nancy Bruning Levine
WOK COOKERY
WOVEN TAPESTRIES

Marilyn Nierenberg
ZOETROPES

Mary Grace Skurka
YARN PAINTING
YO-YOS

Originating editor of the series:
Allen Davenport Bragdon

Contributing editor:
Dennis Starin

Contributing photographers:
Henry Chu
Steven Mays
Dennis Starin

Contributing illustrators:
Martin Abrahams
Marina Givotovsky
Paul Killian
Patricia Lee
Lynn Matus
Sally Shimizu

Production:
Thom Augusta
Christopher Jones
Sylvia Sherwin
Leslie Strong

Photo and illustration credits:
YARN PAINTING: Photograph, page 2910, courtesy of The Mexican Art Annex, New York, N.Y. Yarns for clown portrait, page 2913, paper plate mask, page 2914, and shampoo-bottle yarn painting, page 2917: Brunscraft Bulky Multicraft Yarn by Brunswick Worsted Mills, Inc., 230 Fifth Avenue, New York, N.Y., and Dritz Quickpoint Yarn by Scovill Manufacturing Company, Sewing Notions Division, 350 Fifth Avenue, New York, N.Y. Yarns for landscape with feathers, page 2916: The 9-Color Yarn by William Unger & Co., Inc., 230 Fifth Avenue, New York, N.Y.; Dritz Quickpoint Yarn; Danish Bulky Yarn by Emile Bernat & Sons Co., Uxbridge, Mass., and Veloura needlepoint yarn by Idle Hands, Kew Gardens, N.Y. ZOETROPES: Praxinoscope, page 2926, early thaumatrope, page 2927, and zoetrope, page 2934, from the collection of Alan and Hillary Weiner, New York. Phenakistoscope wheels, page 2930, courtesy of Joel Kopp, America Hurrah Antiques, New York, N.Y. *Pow!*, picture strip, page 2938, designed by Paul Killian. Flipbook, page 2942, courtesy of Martin Abrahams.

The Project-Evaluation Symbols appearing in the title heading at the beginning of each project have these meanings:

Range of approximate cost:

¢ Low: under $5 or free and found natural materials

$ Medium: about $10

$$ High: above $15

Estimated time to completion for an unskilled adult:

⊠ Hours

🕐 Days

📅 Weeks

Suggested level of experience:

🧒 Child alone

👥 Supervised child or family project

🧍 Unskilled adult

🧍 Specialized prior training

Tools and equipment:

⚒ Small hand tools

🔨 Large hand and household tools

⚗ Specialized or powered equipment

On the cover:
This vibrantly colored tree-of-life design by Sonja Douglas was inspired by a traditional motif of the Polish paper-cutting craft, wycinanki. Instructions for this technique begin on page 2888. Photograph by Paul Levin.

**Contents and
Craftspeople for
Volume 23:**

WIRE SCULPTURE
Bent for Beauty

For contemporary artists and craftsmen, wire has become the medium for making a wide range of useful and beautiful jewelry and other art objects. Since wire has such wide technological applications, it is available in an incredible variety of shapes, thicknesses (called gauges), colors, and materials. This diversity provides craftsmen with a medium rich for creative exploration.

Wire is an ancient material, and how it is worked has changed little over the centuries. Today's wires are of more consistent quality, and tools have been refined, but the basic techniques of bending, forging, and annealing remain the same. For the most part, tools needed for working wire are few and inexpensive, and techniques used are readily mastered.

Materials and Tools

Most metals are available as wire. Precious metals—silver, gold, and platinum—yield expensive wire. But inexpensive wire of copper, brass, or aluminum is worked in almost precisely the same manner as the precious metals and can be used for any of the projects shown on the pages that follow. Usually many kinds of scrap wire can be found around the home or can be had for the asking from neighbors, businesses, or junkyards. Wire is also available at hardware stores and crafts supply stores. When you buy wire, you can specify both gauge and shape. Gauge numbers identify thickness; they run in inverse order so the lower the number, the thicker the wire. As to shape, round wire is the most prevalent form, but square, oval, or half-round wire is also available.

Wire working requires few special tools. Hand manipulation without tools is possible in many instances, but for precise bending and for handling heavy wires, you will need pliers. Most useful are needle-nosed and flat-nosed types. When you choose pliers, avoid those with toothed jaws that would leave marks on the wire. If smooth-jawed pliers are not available, cover the teeth with masking tape.

Jigs, devices used for shaping wire, can be time-savers when you are making a series of identical or similar parts. Commercial jigs for forming, twisting, and bending wire are often inexpensive. But most craftsmen find that homemade jigs work just as well. Bowls and tin cans of various diameters can be used to shape coils or rings; nails driven into a block of wood serve to define more intricate forms.

Thin wire is readily cut with old scissors or nail clippers. Cutting thicker or harder wire requires investment in a pair of wire nippers or shears that will yield a clean cut. Piano wire and coat-hanger wire, for example, are not easy to use unless you can cut them easily.

Jay Hartley Newman (left), a graduate of Columbia University School of Law, and Lee Scott Newman (right), a graduate student in psychology at Cornell University, are the authors of Wire Art, Kite Craft, *and* Plastics for the Craftsman. *With Thelma R. Newman, they have written* Paper as Art and Craft, The Frame Book, *and* The Lamp Book.

Interlocking loops and semicircles of brass wire are simple to shape and assemble, but they result in a delicate neckpiece.

Jewelry, Lapidary, and Metalwork
Looped-link necklace

The necklace shown at right is made by bending wire into uniform loops that are hooked to each other. Two weights of wire are used. Tools you will need are: wire cutters; needle-nosed pliers (with jaws that come to a fine, round point); a fine file; a bench vise; and 400-grit wet-or-dry sandpaper. A motorized buffing wheel for polishing is useful, though not essential. The necklace shown was executed in brass, with No. 1 gauge wire in the neck ring and No. 23 gauge wire in the loops. This design could be worked in a variety of metals, including silver, gold, copper, or silver plated wire. The thickness of the wires could also be varied. Twelve-gauge wire, for example, is heavy enough to be used for the neck ring but flexible enough for the loops. Regardless of the gauge or kind of metal, the process is the same.

A two-headed, four-armed, four-footed monster, breathing fire, was a denizen of the craftsman's imagination until he was portrayed in wrapped 18-gauge aluminum wire.

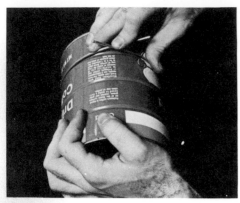

1: Begin the necklace by bending the wire for the neck ring around a large coffee can, 5 inches in diameter, used as a jig. Allow a 2-inch overlap where the ends meet.

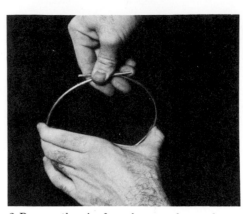

2: Remove the wire from the can and press the overlapping ends firmly together to close the circle, being careful to maintain the circular shape of the can.

3: Place the wire in a bench vise. Using a jeweler's saw, cut the overlapping wire so there will be a 2-inch gap in the neck ring. This allows the ring to be slipped on and off easily.

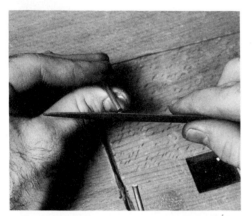

4: Using a fine file, remove any jagged burrs left on the cut ends of the ring. Then file the cut ends until they are rounded so the ring can be slipped on the neck without scratching.

5: Using 400-grit wet-or-dry sandpaper dipped in water, sand the two filed ends until all file marks have been removed. Use the moist sandpaper to remove any other mars from the ring.

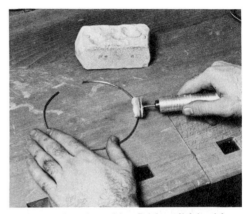

6: To give the wire a shiny finish, polish it with a motorized buffing wheel of cloth, using a block of jeweler's white compound as a fine abrasive. Or simply apply the abrasive with a rag.

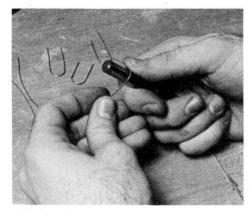

7: To form the small U shapes at the top of the necklace, use a marking pen or small screwdriver handle as a shaping jig. Such jigs permit you to make any number of parts of a uniform size.

8: A hammer handle or a large turned finial like this makes a good jig for forming the larger semi-circles that are joined to form the triangular pendant of the necklace.

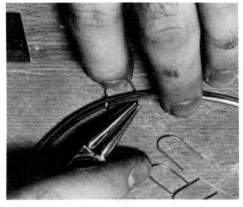

9: To attach the U-shaped loops to the neck wire, bend the ends of the lighter wire into hooks; then squeeze the hooks around the heavier wire with needle-nosed pliers until it fits snugly.

Begin with an 18-inch piece of the neck-ring wire. To turn this straight piece of wire into a perfect circle, use a large coffee can, 5 inches in diameter, as a jig. Try not to mar the surface of the wire, since any nick or scratch will have to be filed, sanded, and buffed away later. Bend the wire around the can until it has assumed a symmetrical, circular shape (photograph 1). Then take the wire off the can and press the overlapping ends together (photograph 2). The overlap may seem wasteful, but it permits you to form the ends of the neck ring accurately.

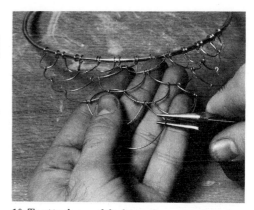

10: To attach one of the larger loops, use the same technique as before to wrap its ends around the wires above it, squeezing the hooks until they are closed. Follow the design shown in Figure A.

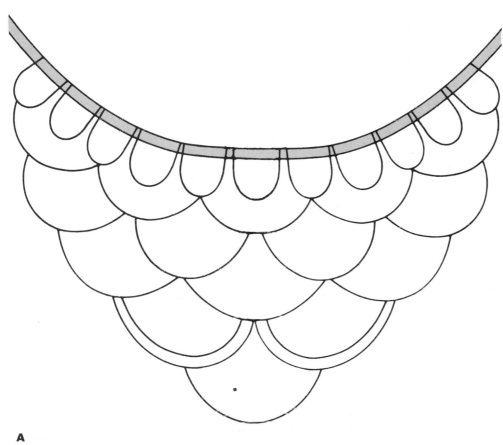

A

Figure A: Follow this full-sized drawing as you shape and position the triangle of small and large loops that is suspended from a neck ring in the necklace.

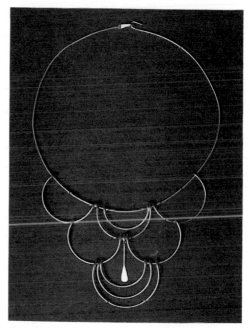

A variation of the necklace of interlocking loops described here is made of 16-gauge silver-plated wire. The center element near the bottom is a short length of wire with one end hammered until the wire is flat; the other end is hooked onto the wire loop above it.

So this ring can be slipped on and off easily, clamp the ring in a vise and cut off the overlapping wire so you leave a 2-inch gap in the circle (photograph 3). Make the cuts with a jeweler's saw; then use a fine file to remove any burrs at the cut ends. File the ends until they are rounded (photograph 4). Next, wet-sand the two ends until all file marks are removed (photograph 5). Dip 400-grit wet-or-dry sandpaper in water occasionally to keep it lubricated. This is also the time to remove any dents or scratches in the wire's surface. To produce a very glossy finish, polish the neck ring with a motorized buffing wheel made of cloth using a block of jeweler's white compound as the abrasive (photograph 6). To get a good shine without a buffing wheel, sand any previously sanded areas again, using 600-grit sandpaper (a finer grit), then apply the appropriate metal polish with a soft cloth. Repeat the sanding and polishing until all blemishes disappear. Wipe away excess polishing compound with a damp cloth.

To shape the two sizes of uniform loops that dangle from the neck ring, you will need to improvise jigs. Rounded handles of hammers and screwdrivers, dowels, screw-on jar lids, or even the barrel of a marking pen all make good mini-jigs. Cut the wire into eleven 2-inch lengths for the small loops and seventeen 3-inch lengths for the larger ones. One by one, center the short pieces on a small jig and bend them around it, forming U shapes (photograph 7). Using needle-nosed pliers, bend small hooks at the ends of each U shape, perpendicular to the loop itself. Do not close these hooks all the way until you are actually interlinking the loops. Use a larger jig to bend the 17 larger semicircles (photograph 8). Then you are ready to interlink the necklace, following Figure A. Begin by attaching the 11 small loops directly to the neck ring (photograph 9) by bending the hooks closed around the ring with the pliers. Then add successive rows of the larger loops, using the same technique (photograph 10). This is only one of many necklace designs you could make. The number, shape, and arrangement of loops are infinitely variable.

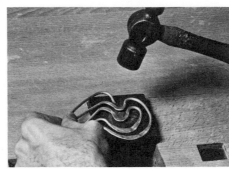

There are several metal-working techniques that are particularly well suited for wire sculpture. Most call for the use of pliers or hammers. All tools used for working wire should be smooth so they do not leave unwanted marks in the wire. Pliers with grooves or teeth in their jaws can be made usable by wrapping each jaw with surgical or masking tape (above).

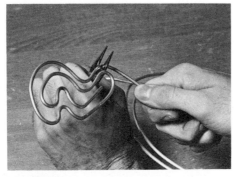

Bending
Bending (above) is the fundamental wire-working technique. Any wire can be bent, either by hand, with pliers, or around a jig.

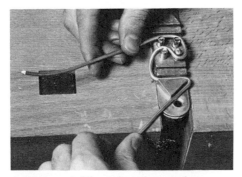

A commercial jig such as the one shown above, clamped in a vise, is available at tool, hardware, and craft supply stores. Jigs are useful in making bends in a variety of shapes. Bends can range from smooth, gentle curves to sharp angles, in either two or three dimensions.

Forging
Forging is the process of shaping wire by hammering it against a hard surface, usually a steel block or anvil (above). Different hammers create different textures. A hammer with a curved surface (ball peen hammer) is used to shape, raise, and curve wire; a flat-surfaced hammer is used to flatten metal. Some wires can be flattened more than others without breaking, depending on the physical characteristics. Always clean both the hammer and the anvil before forging; otherwise dirt may be embedded in the wire. Begin flattening the wire slowly, tapping it lightly. If you strike a quick, heavy blow, expecting to finish the job quickly, you may split the wire. Hammer both sides of the wire. At some point, the hammering will cease to have any flattening effect; the wire has been made hard and brittle and it needs to be annealed.

Annealing
Annealing relieves stresses and strains caused by bending and forging; it is achieved by applying heat to the wire. Experiment first to determine the tolerance of the wire being used; see how far you can forge it before it cracks with brittleness. To soften metal becoming brittle before it cracks, heat the wire with a portable propane torch (above). Place the bent wire on an asbestos pad or other fireproof material. Focus the blue tip of the flame so it just touches a section of the wire until the metal glows a dull red for a second or two. Repeat along the entire length; then let the wire

cool. Annealing the wire in this manner restores malleability, but it usually leaves a coating of oxides on the surface. These oxides can be removed with a solution called pickle.

Pickling
Pickle is lukewarm, diluted acid. To make it, dissolve sodium bisulfate, a granular dry acid compound, in warm water according to the package directions. For safety's sake, avoid touching the acid solution or inhaling the fumes. If your skin is sensitive, wear rubber gloves. Soak the annealed wire in the bath for several minutes (above) until the oxides disappear or can be rubbed off with a cloth. Remove the wire with tongs made of copper, brass, or nickel, but never of iron or steel. Wash the wire in soapy water; then dry it. After annealing the forging may be repeated; the wire can be flattened a bit more without fear of its breaking. Forging, heating, and pickling can be repeated a number of times, depending on the gauge and kind of wire being used. Eventually, however, any wire will reach its limit and break.

Clumping
Clumping is a means of binding groups of wire so you can cut short, equal pieces of wire. Fold a single length of wire back and forth until you have the desired number of wires. Wind another piece of wire around the center to secure the bundle. Then clip the folded ends with a wire cutter (above).

WIRE WORKING

Crumpling
Crumpling is a way of bunching wire to make a desired shape. Squeeze loosely gathered wire in your hands (above) until it becomes the size and shape you want.

Braiding
Braiding wire is much like braiding yarn. First hammer three finishing nails side by side into the end of a board, and loop a double strand of wire around each. Bring the right wire across the center wire, then the left wire across the center wire, and so forth (above). Some wires are easier to braid than others, depending on their flexibility. You can experiment with single, double, and multistrand braids.

Twisting
Twisting is a basic method of attaching wires together. Soft wires may be twisted by hand, using a pencil to hold the end loop (above).

Wires need not be of the same gauge or even material to be twisted together. Attach one end of the wires to a nail, the other to a pencil, and turn the pencil until the amount of twisting desired is achieved.

Weaving
Wires can be woven together the same way as other fibers, on or off a loom. Shown above is the start of a woven basket. All wires are not equally suited to weaving. Choose soft, flexible wire for the weft and a more rigid wire for the warp or spokes. Weave the softer wire over one spoke, then under the next. Be sure to start with an odd number of spokes when you weave a basket.

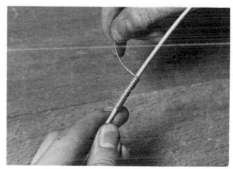

Wrapping
Wrapping is the technique of covering one wire with another wire. A thin wire can be used to cover a heavier wire completely (above).

Characteristics of wire:

Hardness
Hardness is the measure of how easily the surface of the metal can be scratched, dented, or pitted. It is important because the condition of the wire in a finished project determines the beauty of the piece. Aluminum and copper are relatively soft, iron is hard. But any metal can be hardened by forging.

Malleability
Malleability is the capacity of the metal for being hammered flat without cracking or splitting. It can be determined by experimenting with a scrap piece. Gold is the most malleable of metals; it can be forged into foil five-millionths of an inch thick. The malleability of wires, in decreasing order: gold, silver, aluminum, copper, tin, platinum, lead, zinc, iron.

Ductility
Ductility is the capacity of a metal for being drawn into a wire. The more ductile a metal, the finer the wire possible. The ductility of wires, in descending order: gold, silver, platinum, iron, copper, aluminum, zinc, tin, lead.

Tensile strength
Tensile strength is a measurement of the stress a wire can withstand when being pulled from both ends. For example, copper has ten times the tensile strength of tin.

Rigidity
Rigidity is the opposite of malleability. Wire often must be rigid enough to hold a particular shape. Increased rigidity can be created by forging.

Shape
Wire is available in round, half-round, square, and flat shapes. Many gauges (thicknesses) are available with each of these shapes.

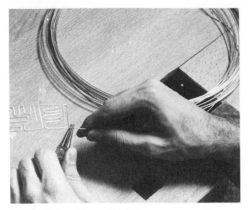

11: Working with a coil of wire, you can continue bending the wire, following any design, until you achieve the length you want.

12: To forge the wire in the belt or bracelet, place it on a clean steel block and hammer various parts of the design until you are pleased with the effect. Every inch should receive at least a few light taps to harden the metal.

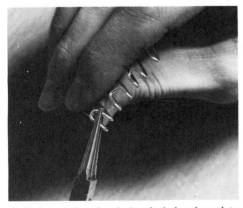

13: To form a clasp for closing the belt or bracelet, make hooks by bending the wires at one end of the piece with a needle-nosed pliers. These hooks slip over a vertical wire at the other end.

Jewelry, Lapidary, and Metalwork
Forged belt and bracelet

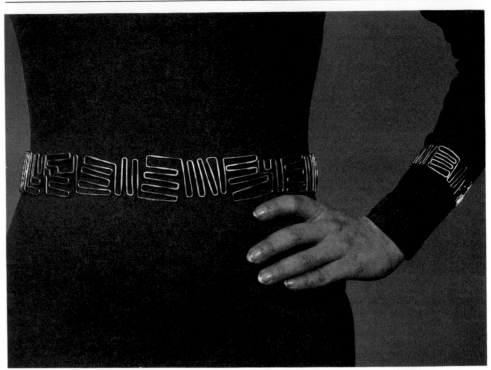

This smart-looking combination of belt and bracelet is made of aluminum wire, carefully bent to form the geometric pattern, and then forged with a hammer to harden and texture it.

Wire bending and forging (hammering the wire against a flat steel surface) together comprise a simple and exciting technique. Using needle-nosed pliers, a ball peen hammer, a metal block, and a propane torch, as detailed in the Craftnotes on pages 2826 and 2827, you can make thousands of wire objects, including the belt-and-bracelet combination shown above.

About 17 feet of wire is needed to make a belt 2 inches wide and 25 inches long because the wire is doubled back and forth to form the design. The bracelet requires 3 feet of wire for its 6-inch length. In other designs, the amount of wire needed will vary. Almost any kind of metal wire can be used. These pieces were executed in 18-gauge aluminum. (Aluminum soils your hands, but this residue can easily be washed off with soap and water.)

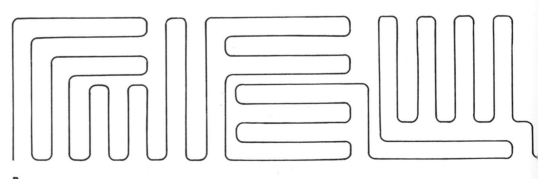

B

Figure B: This pattern, only one of a limitless number possible, shows how the wire was bent to make the belt and bracelet pictured above.

Use smooth-jawed needle-nosed pliers to bend the design of the belt (photograph 11). Follow the pattern in Figure B or create your own. After bending, gently hammer all the wire (photograph 12). This slight forging makes the metal less flexible and imparts a slight curve to the form. Strike every point along the wire just hard enough to slightly flatten the belt surface. Then, for aesthetic reasons, you may want to do more forging on some sections. But every inch should receive at least a few light taps of the hammer to keep the belt (or the bracelet) from stretching out of shape when worn. The forging hammer should have a smooth, flat, unpitted surface, because any mark in its face would be transferred to the wire. A nail hammer's face is slightly rounded; it will not work as well. Forging should be done on a clean, smooth anvil or a flat steel block. The initial forging can be followed by annealing—the application of heat from a propane torch to the wire (Craftnotes, pages 2826 and 2827). This heat softens the metal so it can be further forged without cracking. If only slight flattening is desired, annealing may be omitted. Once the belt and bracelet have been forged, bend the wires at one end into hooks so you can fasten the ends together (photograph 13).

Jewelry, Lapidary, and Metalwork
Meandering forged necklace

Individual lengths of copper wire were bent and forged, then joined to each other with tiny loops to form this necklace. A large angular motif forms the central design.

The bending and forging technique described on the opposite page can be used to make a softer, rounder design like that of the linked necklace shown at right. By hammering longer at certain points, you can vary the amount of flatness achieved with a soft metal like copper. This variation becomes an essential element of the design.

The same tools are used: hammer, pliers, metal block, propane torch. A piece of scrap wood and finishing nails are needed to make a wire-bending jig. And you need 10 feet of 14- or 16-gauge copper wire.

The necklace has 12 identical links plus a center piece and a clasp. These pieces are shown in Figures C, D, and E. To build a jig for shaping the link (Figure C),

C
Figure C. This pattern shows the shape of the wavy link that was repeated 12 times around the necklace, pictured above, right.

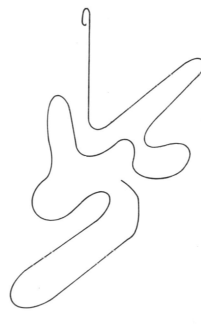

D
Figure D: This is the shape of the large motif, also made of copper wire, that is suspended from the middle of the necklace. You can experiment with other designs or shape your initial with the wire if you prefer.

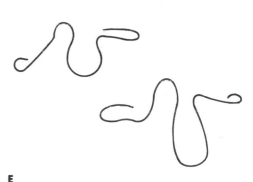

E
Figure E: These two links, with a loop at one end and a U-shaped bend at the other, form the clasp at the back of the necklace.

14: To start a wire necklace, sketch a design like that in Figure C (page 2829) on paper; then copy it onto a wood block. (A connecting loop is formed by wrapping the wire around the end nail.)

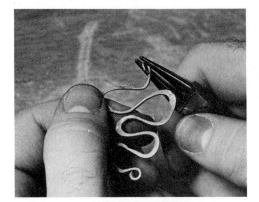

15: Hammer finishing nails into the wood to rim the loops of the penciled pattern. This creates a jig you can use for bending 12 identical links for the necklace.

16: Bend a piece of wire around the nails so the wire assumes the shape of the pattern. Use a screwdriver to help press the wire snugly around the intricate curves.

17: Using wire cutters, snip off the excess wire at the ends of the shaped link.

18: Using needle-nosed pliers, adjust the small loop at each end so there is a space enclosed by the loop. This will be hooked to a loop of the next link when you assemble the necklace.

19: Each of the links can be forged with a hammer and steel block, some of them more so than others. Test a piece of the wire so you know how much you can hammer it before it cracks.

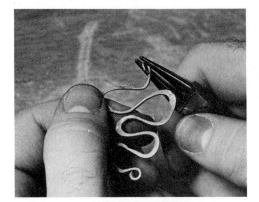

20: After forging the links, use the pliers to turn one of the end loops perpendicular to the link so it can be attached to the next link.

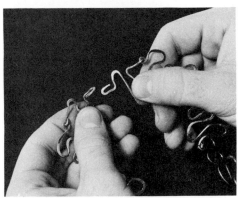

21: The two clasp pieces, patterned in Figure E, are attached to the ends of the necklace. They are designed to be easily closed or opened.

sketch it first on paper; then copy the drawing on the surface of a block of wood (photograph 14). Drive finishing nails into the wood along the penciled line (photograph 15). To make a link, bend a 7- or 8-inch length of the wire around the nails (photograph 16). At each end of the link, wrap the wire around the last nail to form a loop for joining the links. Remove the bent wire from the jig and snip off any excess wire (photograph 17). With the pliers, adjust the small loops (photograph 18). Next, forge each link as you like, using a hammer and metal block (photograph 19). But rather than flattening the entire link, experiment by forging some parts and not others or by forging some areas more than others. If the wire becomes hard and brittle, you can anneal the link to soften it (Craftnotes, pages 2826 and 2827). Polish each link with a buffing wheel (a buffing disk attached to an electric drill) or with copper polish and a soft cloth. Turn one loop at the end of each link perpendicular to the rest of the link so that the links can be joined together smoothly (photograph 20). Make a larger, more elaborate bent and forged piece for the center of the necklace (Figure D, page 2829). Then make small hooks, bent and forged, to serve as clasps at the back (Figure E, page 2829). Polish these pieces as well. Assemble the necklace by fitting the links together, with the larger piece in the center and a clasp piece at each end. A close-up view of the clasp is shown in photograph 21.

Jewelry, Lapidary, and Metalwork
Spring flowers and eucalyptus

Flowers and eucalyptus branches that will never wilt are made of copper and brass wire (the flowers) and florist's wire with shaped green plastic tiles for leaves (the branches).

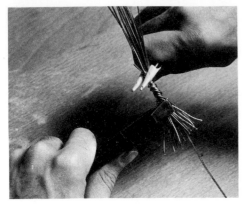

22: Use a pair of pliers to hold petal wires as you twist them together with a second pair of pliers until all, including the projecting stem wire, are securely held together.

23: To form the coiled petals, spread out the individual wires; then wrap each wire separately around a screwdriver shaft, dowel, or pencil. Wrap the wire close to itself to form a tight coil.

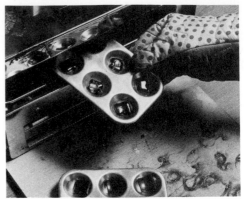

24: To turn green plastic squares into rounded leaves, place the tiles in muffin tins and slide them into a 325-degree oven. As the tiles begin to melt, remove them from the oven.

25: To string the cooled and shaped tiles on florist's wire, heat the tip of the wire in a candle flame; then push the tile quickly down the wire to the place where you want it to stay.

The striking floral bouquet shown on page 2831 is constructed of many lengths of copper and brass wire plus colorful plastic mosaic tiles (the eucalyptus leaves) strung on florist's wire.

To make each flower, cut 12 to 18 individual strands of a soft wire 12 to 18 inches long. The more strands you use, the fuller the flower blossom will be. The flowers pictured are made of 20-gauge copper and brass wire, but thinner or thicker wire could be used. Cut a single 12-inch strand of heavier wire (14 gauge) to serve as the stem. Letting the stem project from the bundle of finer wires, use one pair of pliers to grip all the strands at the point where the stem and flower strands meet. Allowing a 2-inch overlap, use a second pair of pliers to twist the strands and stem wire together until they are firmly joined (photograph 22). Carefully spread the strands; then wind each individual flower wire into a tight coil (photograph 23). A screwdriver shaft, pencil, or dowel will serve as a jig for wrapping the coil. Wrap the stem wire with green waxed florist's tape to complete the blossom. Make as many of these flowers as you would like in your bouquet; the one pictured has nine.

The eucalyptus branches are constructed of green florist's wire and ¾-inch-square plastic mosaic tiles. This bouquet has five 12-inch branches, each with about a dozen leaves. Shape the tiles by melting them in an oven or broiler at 325 degrees Fahrenheit until they sag into the paint cups or muffin tins that serve as molds (photograph 24). Then remove the tiles from the heat. The tiles harden into the curved shape and do not stick to the pan. After you remove them from the oven, using an insulated glove to avoid burns, set them aside to cool.

To string the tiles onto the florist's wire, heat just the tip of the wire stem in the flame of a candle or stove burner. When the tip is hot, it will pierce the plastic tile (photograph 25). Slide the tile quickly down the wire stem and allow it to cool in the position where you want it to stay. Place the wire flowers in a vase and arrange the plastic eucalyptus leaves around them. The wires are flexible and can be bent if necessary until a pleasing arrangement is achieved.

A small wire basket has forged copper-wire spokes woven with color-coated copper wire and brass wire. A variety of colors can be introduced in such a project by using different wires.

Jewelry, Lapidary, and Metalwork
Wire basket

Wire, just like raffia, straw, or jute, can be woven to make a basket. To begin you need a skeleton of spokes around which to weave. In the basket shown at left, there are eight 18-inch-long spokes of 16-gauge copper wire. The finished basket is 4 inches tall. The spokes are purposely cut long to allow some flexibility in shaping the basket; they will be neatly trimmed off after the weaving is completed.

Before you assemble the skeletal shape, forge each of the spokes (photograph 26). This hardens the wire so it will not stretch out of shape. Then lay the forged spokes in a sunburst pattern with all the spokes crossing in the center. Arrange the

26: To make a basket of copper wire, cut the spokes of heavy wire and forge each by hammering it on a steel plate. This will prevent the wire from stretching during the weaving process.

27: Arrange the forged spokes in a sunburst pattern, crossing them at the center. Tie them together with fine, flexible wire passed between each pair of adjacent spokes.

28: Using wire cutters, cut off half of one spoke so you are left with an odd number of spokes. This is necessary for weaving in a circle. Adjust the spokes slightly so the spacing is even.

29: Begin weaving where the spokes cross, using a fine, flexible wire. Once the spokes are secure, you can add other wires for color and texture. Here, a heavier brass wire is being introduced.

30: When the weaving is completed, bend the spokes toward the center of the basket and cut them off ¼ inch from the basket edge; then bend these ends down against the side of the basket.

31: Stitch around the top edge of the basket with fine wire to secure the weaving so it will not unravel. Pull each stitch tight and conceal the end under the last stitches.

spokes so there is equal distance between them; then tie them together at the center with very fine 26-gauge coated copper wire (photograph 27). This wire will also be used to start the weaving. Tying the spokes, with a wire through each opening, makes beginning the weave easier because the spokes will not slide together. After tying the spokes, you need to cut off one-half of one spoke and adjust the spacing (photograph 28). In order to weave in a circle you always need an odd number of spokes.

Begin weaving at the center, using a very flexible fine wire that will fit snugly into the spaces between spokes. The color-coated copper wire was used here both for its flexibility and its red color. Once the weaving is under way and the spokes are secure, other wires may be added for variation in color and texture. In the basket shown, 24-gauge brass wire was used (photograph 29). Make sure any cut ends are on the inside of the basket.

Shape the basket as the weaving progresses. The shape of the forged copper spokes largely determines the shape of the basket; so bend these wires to match the shape you want the basket to take. The shape will also be determined by how tautly you pull the wires during the weaving. The tighter the weaving, the more it will pull the spokes together, and the narrower the basket will be.

To finish the basket, bend the projecting copper spokes toward the center of the basket, and snip them off ¼ inch in from the basket rim (photograph 30). Then bend the end of the spokes down into the basket, using pliers. Finally, stitch around the entire top edge with a fine flexible wire, such as the 26-gauge coated copper wire used at the beginning (photograph 31). This top stitching secures the spokes and the weave and prevents the basket from unraveling.

This contemporary Indian basket is woven of forged and unforged brass wire in various weights. The cover is attached to the basket with a wire hinge.

Wire fantasy figures

The mustachioed wiry beast shown below and the one breathing fire on page 2822 are products of imagination visualized with wire. Each figure is constructed around a core of individual wires, bound together with one long piece of wire. To begin any figure, sketch a design—three hands, four feet, eight toes, five heads—almost anything is possible. But you must plan ahead so you will have enough individual wires running through the form to make the limbs and digits desired.

A creature from the fantastic world of the imagination is this mustachioed, 12-footed, long-necked, beady-eyed beauty.

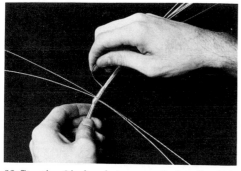

32: Starting 8 inches down, wrap the bundle of 21 wires (six for the head and 15 for the body) with another wire for ½ inch; then pull aside two leg wires on each side and continue wrapping.

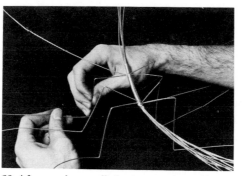

33: After you have pulled out a second set of four legs and have continued the body wrap, bend each leg in two places to form joints. The figure will stand on these legs.

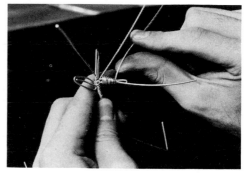

34: After you have shaped the ears and have pulled the eye wires aside, fold one of the remaining wires to form the snout, and wrap it with the remaining wire.

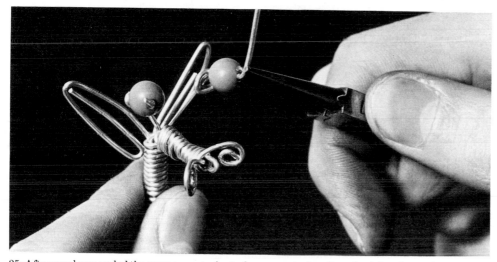

35: After you have curled the excess snout wire to form a mustache, slip a plastic bead on each of the eye wires. Bend the end of the wire to hold the bead in place and snip off the excess.

To construct the 12-legged beast shown opposite, start with 21 one-yard lengths of 18-gauge aluminum wire. This allows six wires for the head, 12 for the legs, and three for the tail. To begin, align six wires for the head. Eight inches down from the end of these wires, position the other 15 wires. Begin wrapping the central core where they meet, using wire long enough to wrap the entire body. Wind it very tightly to secure the wires. This starting point is where the torso begins; construct the body first, the neck and head later. Wrap a ½-inch section; then pull out two wires on each side of the body for the front set of four legs and continue wrapping (photograph 32). Continue wrapping the body, pulling out four wires for the center legs and four wires for the back legs. Then wrap 3 inches more to complete the body. Bend the leg wires so each leg has two joints (photograph 33). (You can snip off excess wire after the figure is completed.) The final three wires are the tail; let them extend beyond the body wrapping.

At the front end, wrap the six wires to form the neck. When the neck is as long as you want it—this one is 4½ inches—separate two of the wires to make the ears. Bend the wire to ear length; then bend it again and snip off the excess. Separate the next two wires for the eyes and leave these free while you finish the snout (photograph 34). Take one of the two remaining wires and bend it around itself to snout length. With the other wire, wrap the length of the snout. To make the mustache, use the excess of the snout wires, curling them under. To finish the eyes, slip a small plastic bead on each eye wire. Bend the wire up to keep the bead from slipping off and snip off the excess (photograph 35). Similar techniques were used to make the two-headed, four-armed, four-footed figure on page 2822.

For related crafts and projects, see "Jewelry," "Pewtersmithing," "Repoussé and Chased Metal," "Silversmithing," "String Art," and "Tin and Pierced Work."

WOK COOKERY

A Taste of China

Fran Shinagel is a superlative cook in many cuisines—Chinese, French, Italian, and several others. Long after she had mastered Continental cooking, she studied Chinese cooking at a New York Chinese cooking school. She was pleased with its adaptability and prepared so many Chinese dishes that eventually her children clamored for hamburger and french fries. Fran finds Chinese and French cuisine quite comparable, in that both are designed to please the eye as well as the palate with various textures, tastes, and colors.

Flavor, aesthetics, and nutrition are blended in a unique way in Chinese cooking. At first glance, this style seems complex, but it has an elegant simplicity and logic. This is especially true when the cooking centers in a wok—a versatile round-bottomed circular cooking pan. Once you learn the fundamental cooking style, you can easily and quickly produce a great variety of authentic Chinese dishes. You need few exotic ingredients or utensils, but you do need a basic understanding of Chinese cooking methods. Pages that follow will describe four types—stir-frying, steaming, deep frying, and sautéing. These methods are quite different but they have one thing in common. The food cooks very quickly. One result is that the food is very nutritious; quick-cooking does not destroy the natural juices of the meats and vegetables. Too, the food is very tasty; meats remain exceedingly tender, and the tender-crisp vegetables retain their flavors and colors. Ideally, you should use fresh, young ingredients. But part of the art of Chinese cooking lies in knowing which method is best for whatever cooking must be done. I have used leftovers many times to concoct dishes with a Chinese flavor.

Utensils

All of the dishes described here can be prepared with utensils you will find familiar. But they can't be compared with the stability and versatility of the two basic Chinese utensils, the wok and the cleaver. Both are inexpensive and easy to use, and both are available in Chinese hardware and food shops.

The wok, pictured on page 2839, is an all-purpose, round cooking pan made of thin metal. It can be used for stir-frying, steaming, sautéing, or deep frying. Round-bottomed and flat-bottomed woks are available. If you buy a round-bottomed wok, it will come with a collar—a ring-shaped device that you can set the wok on to keep it level. It will also come with its own lid. The best size to get for preparing a family meal has a 12- or 14-inch diameter. If you have a gas range, you can turn the burner plate over and use it to cradle a round-bottomed wok in the flame. Or you can remove the burner plate, place the collar over the burner, and set the wok on it. With an electric range, you will need to use a flat-bottomed wok or more conventional utensils. To obtain the heat these recipes require, turn the heating unit up to high. When you need to lower the temperature, remove the pan from the heat for a while; then replace it to raise the heat again. You need high heat—so avoid using an electric wok, since it seldom produces the degree of heat required.

A wok, like a heavy cast-iron pan, needs to be seasoned the first time it is used. This seals the metal and keeps food from sticking to it. To season a wok, wash and dry it; then pour in about two tablespoons of oil and heat until the oil becomes very thin. Tilt the pan so you coat the sides with hot oil. Be careful to avoid burns. Then let the wok cool. Pour off the oil that remains and wipe the inside of the wok with a paper towel, leaving just a light coating. Once you have seasoned the wok, never scour it. To clean it, wash it and dry it immediately; then heat it on the range for a few seconds. That will dry it completely and prevent rusting.

Clockwise, starting from the top, are spicy cabbage, beef with broccoli, deep-fried duck, and steamed sea bass with black bean sauce. These four very different dishes, shown with salt-and-pepper dip and soy-sauce dip, can be cooked in a wok, the versatile Chinese cooking pan. Learn to prepare each dish separately; then serve them at a single meal for four with individual bowls of rice and a pot of hot tea.

Cooking rice

Unlike Western-style rice, which is prepared so it is light and fluffy, Chinese-style rice is intended to be sticky so it will be easy to pick up with chopsticks.

To achieve this, put 1 cup of long-grain white rice in a small saucepan. Rinse it repeatedly with cold water until the water runs clear. Drain completely, and then add 2 cups of water for cooking. In a Chinese kitchen, no measures are used. The rice is simply covered with water; then the tip of the thumb is inserted until it touches the rice. If the water comes up to the first knuckle, it is sufficient.

Cover the pan tightly and place it over high heat. Bring to a boil; then lower the heat for 1 minute. Bring to a boil once more; then lower the heat again and cook for 20 minutes. Remove the rice from the heat, still covered, and let it stand undisturbed for up to 30 minutes. Traditionally, rice is not served piping hot. (Serves four.)

Basic marinade:

¼ cup soy sauce
¼ cup dry sherry
1 teaspoon sugar
1 tablespoon grated fresh ginger (1 teaspoon powdered ginger may be substituted)
1 large clove garlic, grated

Combine all ingredients in a small bowl or jar. If you like, you can make this in larger batches to have on hand; the marinade will keep for one week.

If you prefer to use more familiar pots and pans, you will need three types. For stir-frying and sautéing, use a skillet or pan about 12 inches in diameter, made of thin metal so it will heat quickly. It should be deep enough to retain food during stirring. For deep frying, use a pan that is deep enough to hold several inches of oil. For steaming, you will need a pot with a tight lid and a rack to elevate the dish that holds the food. Make sure the pot is large enough to hold the dish with ½ to 1 inch all around between the pot and the edge of the dish.

For cutting and chopping, the Chinese use a cleaver that resembles a butcher's cleaver (opposite). This serves as an all-purpose knife for cutting vegetables and meat. (The large cleaver will cut through poultry bones.) A cleaver speeds preparations; you can also use it to scoop up the cut pieces and transfer them to the wok. I now use it for other types of cooking as well. If you prefer, instead of a cleaver you can use a long, heavy chef's knife with a triangular blade. Whichever you choose, keep the blade very sharp so you can make clean, neat cuts without crushing the food.

As a companion piece to the cleaver, the Chinese often use a 6-inch-thick slice of wood cut from a tree, but you can use any thick cutting board or butcher block.

You will also need bowls and plates to hold the prepared food. And for stirring, scooping, ladling, tasting, and transferring food, you will need a metal spatula, a large metal spoon, a wooden spoon, and a ladle. For steaming rice, use a brass, copper, or enamel-coated steel pot, or an aluminum one with a heavy bottom. It must have a tight lid to contain the steam so the rice will cook properly. Plan to use the same pot every time you cook rice so you can achieve consistent results.

Ingredients

Most Chinese meals can be prepared with few, if any, special Chinese ingredients, although they add a distinctive flavor. Most ingredients can be purchased at a local supermarket. Pork, beef, fish, and poultry are all used in modern Chinese cooking, and almost any vegetable can be used with them in addition to—or in place of—such traditional favorites as bean sprouts, water chestnuts, bamboo shoots, and dried mushrooms. Dried, fermented black beans, soy sauce, and fresh ginger root can be used in small quantities to impart a subtle flavor. These are available in Chinese grocery stores. Also frequently used for seasoning are salt, pepper, fresh garlic, scallions, and sherry. The Chinese use peanut oil for cooking, but any vegetable oil (except olive oil, which is too heavy) can be used. I prefer peanut or corn oil.

Basic Procedures

Through the centuries, the Chinese cook had to cope with a constant shortage of fuel, so the actual cooking of a Chinese dish rarely takes as long as its preparation.

To make things easy, assemble all ingredients before you begin cooking. Cut everything, as directed, in advance. (All ingredients will be diced, shredded, or sliced in comparatively small, uniform pieces so they will cook quickly and evenly.) Also mix the seasonings or sauces in advance and have them ready to be added quickly when they are needed.

Meat should be cut as directed and soaked in the basic marinade (left) for at least ten minutes. Vegetables should be thoroughly cleaned, peeled if the recipe so specifies, and placed in neat piles on a dish. Dried mushrooms, a commonly used ingredient, should be soaked in hot water for at least 15 minutes before they are used. Decide what pots, pans, and other utensils you will need and set them out on the counter. Choose the serving dishes too, and set them out.

Once you have prepared all the ingredients, you are ready to begin cooking. All of the four methods of cooking described here (stir-frying, steaming, deep frying, and sautéing) require high heat; all but steaming require the use of oil for cooking. Once the pan is hot, pour in the specified amount of oil, and heat it until it begins to smoke slightly; then add the rest of the ingredients. When the oil is hot, I often season it with a slice of fresh ginger and a clove of garlic, unpeeled and crushed with the broad side of a cleaver. Remove and discard these when they turn golden brown. To add oil or water during the cooking, pour it down the side of the pan. When you add sauce or gravy, make a hollow in the center of the ingredients, exposing the bottom of the pan, and pour the sauce into the hollow. After the sauce is slightly heated, stir it into the rest of the ingredients.

Kitchen Favorites and Celebrations
Spicy cabbage

¢ ▨ 🚶 🥫

The Chinese invented stir-frying, an ancient cooking method that is still the most popular style of Chinese cooking. The ingredients are cut up into bite-sized pieces, then stirred rapidly for a short time, over high heat, in a small amount of oil. The hot oil preserves the color, texture, and flavor of the ingredients, and seals in the juices and nutrients. The spicy cabbage shown on page 2837 is a stir-fry dish. It requires few ingredients and a minimum of preparation and cooking. It can be served at room temperature or piping hot.

Ingredients:

½ head of cabbage
2 tablespoons vegetable oil
1 slice fresh ginger, unpeeled
1 clove garlic, unpeeled

Sauce:

2 tablespoons sugar
2 tablespoons white vinegar
1 tablespoon soy sauce
Cayenne pepper, hot sauce, or Chinese chili oil, to taste

Preparation
Combine the sauce ingredients in a small bowl. Then cut the cabbage into large chunks (photograph 1) or shred it as for cole slaw. Place the garlic and ginger on your cutting board, and crush them slightly with the flat side of the cleaver.

Cooking
Heat the wok; then add the oil and heat it until it smokes. Add the crushed garlic and ginger, and cook them until they begin to turn golden brown (photograph 2). Then discard them. This imparts just a hint of these flavors to the oil.

With a large spoon, repeatedly scoop up the hot oil, coating the sides of the wok. Then add the cabbage. In the stir-fry method, ingredients must be kept in constant motion. To accomplish this, I use both a large spoon and a large metal spatula (photograph 3). Do this for 2 or 3 minutes; by then each piece of cabbage should be coated with oil. Pour in the previously prepared sauce; then stir and cook the cabbage until each piece is coated with sauce. Remove to a serving dish.

Kitchen Favorites and Celebrations
Beef with broccoli

¢ ▨ 🚶 🥫

1: To prepare cabbage for stir-fry cooking, cut it into quarters with a cleaver and then into large chunks. The leaves will be easy to separate. Keep your fingers away from the sharp blade.

2: To season the hot oil before you add the cabbage, cook one clove of garlic and a slice of ginger, both crushed to release their flavor, until they turn golden brown; then remove them.

3: The stir-fry method of cooking requires that the ingredients be kept in constant motion; use both a large spoon and a spatula to achieve this.

Stir-fried beef with broccoli also contains onions, mushrooms, and cherry tomatoes. The ingredients were chosen for their texture and color, in addition to their flavor—a characteristic of Chinese cooking.

Many wok dishes, like the beef with broccoli shown on page 2839, combine meat with vegetables. This type of recipe is so typical, in fact, that the variations are infinite. Using the procedures described here, you can create your own unique recipes, substituting lamb, ham, or any leftover meat for the beef and frozen peas or another green vegetable for the broccoli. Like the cabbage dish on page 2839, this dish is stir-fried. But it is more complex because each ingredient needs to cook a different length of time. The tough ones that need the most cooking are put into the wok first. Tender ones (which require less cooking) are added later, so at the end everything is ready at the same time. Timing is the key so it is important to have everything prepared and ready to put into the wok when its time comes. Once the cooking begins, you will not have time to search for ingredients.

Ingredients:

½ pound flank steak, skirt steak,
    or chuck filet
Basic marinade (page 2838)
¼ cup vegetable oil
1 slice fresh ginger, unpeeled
1 clove garlic, unpeeled

½ bunch of broccoli
½ large onion
¼ cup dried mushrooms
1 pint cherry tomatoes
½ cup chicken or beef broth
2 teaspoons cornstarch combined with
    2 teaspoons water

Preparation

To make beef with broccoli, first place the dried mushrooms in a small bowl and cover them with hot water. Let them soak for half an hour while you prepare the other ingredients. Trim any fat from the meat; then slice it across the grain. The grain is indicated by the direction of the lines of fat (photograph 4). Slicing will be easier if you have kept the meat in a freezer for about an hour to firm it. Place the sliced meat in the basic marinade; let it soak while you cut up the vegetables.

Wash the broccoli; then cut off the flowerets at the top of the stems (photograph 5). Peel the stalks with a potato peeler or small knife, cut them into 3-inch chunks, and slice them vertically (photograph 6). Place the broccoli on a large plate, keeping the flowerets and the stems separate. Peel the onion and cut it into small chunks, separating the layers as you cut. Place the onion on the plate, keeping it separate from the broccoli. Wash the tomatoes, remove the stems, and place the tomatoes on the vegetable plate. The ingredients at this stage are shown at left.

In a small bowl, blend the cornstarch and water. Remove the meat from the marinade, squeezing it with your hands to remove as much liquid as possible (reserve the marinade). Then put the meat on paper towels and dry it well. If the meat is wet, it will make the hot oil splatter. Remove the softened mushrooms from their soaking liquid, cut off and discard the stems, and add the caps to the vegetable plate. Finally, place the ginger slice and the clove of garlic on the cutting board, and crush them with the flat side of the cleaver.

Cooking

Heat the wok; then pour in the oil and heat it until it begins to smoke. Add the garlic and ginger. Remove and discard them when they turn golden brown.

Put the broccoli stems and onion into the wok, and stir-fry as directed for cabbage (page 2839), cooking about 2 minutes (photograph 7). Then add the broccoli

Timing is critical in making a stir-fried dish such as beef with broccoli, so all ingredients should be prepared before the cooking begins. The plate at left contains the cut-up vegetables; in the bowl at right are pieces of beef soaking in a flavorful marinade.

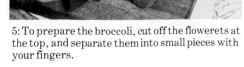

4: To slice beef for wok stir-frying, cut it across the grain into 1-by-3-by-¼-inch pieces. Lines of fat parallel the grain.

5: To prepare the broccoli, cut off the flowerets at the top, and separate them into small pieces with your fingers.

6: Cut the broccoli stalks into 3-inch lengths; then slice each chunk of broccoli stalk vertically into ⅛-inch-thick pieces.

7: Since the broccoli stems and onion require the most cooking, begin cooking them first, stirring constantly.

8: Next, add the softened dried mushrooms and broccoli flowerets, which take less time to cook, again stirring constantly.

9: With the vegetables removed, cook the beef, pressing it flat against the sides of the wok so it sears quickly, but keeping it moving.

flowerets and mushrooms, which take less time to cook, and stir-fry for another 2 minutes (photograph 8). Add the chicken or beef broth to the wok, and cook for about 1 minute more. Using a slotted spoon, remove the vegetables from the wok and place them on a large plate.

Put the marinated beef in the wok (enough oil and broth should remain for cooking it, but if not, add more oil by pouring it down the sides of the wok). Keeping the meat moving, cook it for about 2 minutes (photograph 9).

Add the cooked vegetables to the meat in the wok and toss them together. Add the tomatoes and stir again (photograph 10). Make a well in the center of the ingredients, and pour in the cornstarch mixture, then the reserved marinade. Cook, stirring constantly, for as long as it takes the sauce to thicken and the tomatoes to heat through (about 1 minute). Remove to a covered serving dish and serve immediately, or keep warm in a low-temperature oven until you are ready to serve.

10: Return the vegetables to the wok, mixing them with the meat. Then add the tomatoes and sauce. Each cooking stage takes only a minute or two.

Kitchen Favorites and Celebrations
Steamed fish, black bean sauce ¢ ⊠ 🚼 🍲

This sea bass required only 12 minutes of steaming to reach delicate perfection. Because the fish was steamed, it has remained moist and tender. It was cooked with a flavorful black bean sauce, and garnished with dainty strips of fresh ginger and scallions.

China has more than 3,000 miles of coastline, plus abundant lakes, rivers, and streams. The Chinese consume large quantities of fish, and steamed fish is one of their favorites. If you can resist the temptation to lift the lid and peek during the steaming process, the fish will cook to perfection in a short time, remaining moist and tender without the addition of oil. For this dish, I usually use a small, fresh sea bass or red snapper that has been scaled and cleaned but with head and tail left intact. This makes a dramatic entrée, as shown on page 2841. You can steam any firm-fleshed fresh fish or frozen fish fillet.

Ingredients:

A 1½-pound fresh, whole fish, such as sea bass or red snapper, scaled and cleaned
2 scallions
A walnut-sized piece of fresh ginger

Sauce:
Basic marinade (page 2838)
2 tablespoons fermented black beans

Preparing and Cooking

To make the black bean sauce, wash and mince the beans and add them to the basic marinade. Make several shallow diagonal cuts on both sides of the cleaned fish to allow the sauce to penetrate. Place the fish in a shallow bowl, cover it with sauce, and pour some sauce inside the fish. Let the fish marinate for from 30 minutes to an hour.

Meanwhile, prepare the scallions and ginger. Cut each scallion into thirds (photograph 11). Then slice each section into thin matchstick strips, guiding the cleaver with the knuckles of one hand while you wield it with the other (photograph 12). Leaving the ginger unpeeled, cut it in half; then cut each half into ⅛-inch-thick slices. Place each slice, flat side down, on the board and cut it into matchstick strips (photograph 13). Set aside.

With all ingredients prepared, set up the wok for steaming. There are several kinds of steaming racks, but I find a small tin can, such as a tuna tin, emptied of its contents and with top and bottom removed, works well. Both woks in photograph 14 are ready to be used as steamers. It is only essential that the steam be able to circulate freely. For this, the plate must be elevated enough to provide ½ to 1 inch of space all around between its rim and the sides of the wok.

Pour water into the wok until it comes to 1 inch below the plate. Place the wok over the burner and begin to heat the water.

As the water heats, arrange the strips of scallions and ginger on top of the marinated fish. When the water has come to a vigorous boil, place the fish plate on the rack, sauce and all. Cover the wok tightly with its lid. If you do not have a lid, make one from aluminum foil. Allow the fish to steam until it is done (the size pictured—1½ pounds—takes 12 minutes). Do not remove the lid or foil so that the steam escapes during the cooking period. When the fish is cooked, remove the cover carefully, standing aside to avoid the steam (photograph 15). Using potholders, lift out the plate carefully (it will be very hot). Serve the fish immediately in the dish in which it was cooked.

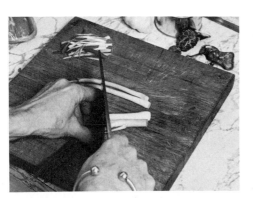

11: To prepare scallions for steamed fish, trim about ¼ inch from each end. Then slice each scallion into thirds, using the entire vegetable.

12: Slice each section of scallion into very thin strips. If you use a cleaver for this kind of slicing, use the knuckles of the free hand to guide the tool as you slice.

13: Cut each half of the fresh ginger into thin slices (left). Then cut each slice into thin strips the same size as the scallions (right).

14: The round-bottomed wok (right) is equipped with a steaming rack. The flat-bottomed wok (left background) holds an empty tin can.

15: When the fish is cooked, lift off the foil cover or lid, (stand out of the way of the escaping steam). Serve the steamed fish in its cooking dish.

Kitchen Favorites and Celebrations
Deep-fried duck

¢ ● 🕴 ☕

Deep frying is a delicious way of preparing duck. As shown at right, the skin is crispy while the meat inside is moist and tender. The preparatory steps can be done a day ahead, and only the frying is left to be done just before serving.

Ingredients:

A 3½-pound duck
Basic marinade (page 2838)
3 scallions, chopped
1 tablespoon five-spices powder
   or allspice

3 cups vegetable oil

Dry dip:

1 tablespoon Szechwan pepper or black
   peppercorns
2 tablespoons coarse salt

Crisp deep-fried duck, cut into serving pieces, is served with a dry salt-and-pepper dip.

Preparation and Cooking

Check to make sure the duck's oil sacs, which are just above the tail, have been removed. If not, cut a slit at the back of the tail and remove them. At least one day before you plan to serve the duck, place it on a flat surface and press down on it with your hand, breaking the backbone and the breastbone to release their flavor. Rub the skin with chopped scallions. Then add the five-spices powder or the allspice to the marinade, put it in a bowl, and let the duck marinate for 3 hours at room temperature or overnight in the refrigerator.

Discard the marinade. With the duck in the same bowl, steam it for 1½ hours (steaming procedures are described and pictured opposite). Turn off the heat and let the duck stand in the covered wok for 15 minutes. Then turn the duck over, replace the cover, and let stand for another 15 minutes. Remove the duck to a plate and let it dry for 3 to 6 hours, or overnight. Do not refrigerate.

One-half hour to 45 minutes before serving, heat the wok. Then pour in the oil and heat it. Meanwhile, prepare the dry dip by placing the salt in a small, heavy pan and toasting it until it is slightly browned. Crush the browned salt and the peppercorns together. To do this, either wrap them in a towel and pound with the flat side of a cleaver, or crush them in a mortar with a pestle, or break them in a blender. Place the dry dip in small individual plates or bowls. When the oil is boiling, carefully slide the whole duck into the wok (photograph 16). Fry it for 10 to 15 minutes on each side, until it is crunchy and golden brown. Move the duck periodically with a large spoon so it doesn't stick to the wok. Occasionally use the spoon to pour hot oil over the top of the duck.

When the duck is done, lift it out of the wok and slide it onto a cutting board. With a cleaver, cut it in half down the center (photograph 17). Then cut the remainder into small pieces for serving (photograph 18). Place these on a serving plate (in China, the pieces would be arranged on the plate in their original positions, in effect reassembling the duck). Place salt-and-pepper dip in front of each diner so each can dip pieces of the duck into it.

16: Slide the duck into boiling oil. The strainer shown is the Chinese tool traditionally used for putting a whole duck into oil.

17: Using a heavy cleaver, you can cut through bones without splintering them to divide the cooked duck in half.

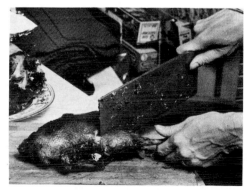

18: Cut each half of the duck into smaller pieces for serving, beginning by removing the legs and the wings.

Uncle Li, as he likes to be called, was born in the Szechwan province of mainland China, where he started cooking when he was fourteen years old. He worked as a chef in Hong Kong for many years, then became a chef at Szechwan Taste, a restaurant in New York's Chinatown.

Kitchen Favorites and Celebrations
Tai Chien chicken

¢ ☒ 🚶 🥘

In Tai Chien Chicken, bite-sized pieces of boneless chicken are cooked with celery, onion, and red or green pepper.

The chicken dish pictured above was named by its originator in honor of Chang Tai Chien, a famous Chinese artist.

Ingredients (serves two):

Approximately 10 ounces of boneless chicken, cut into bite-sized pieces
2 egg yolks, slightly beaten
3 cups vegetable oil
2 stalks celery, cut in ¼-inch-thick diagonal slices
¼ large onion, cut in large chunks
½ red or green pepper, cut into small pieces
1 teaspoon finely chopped fresh ginger
½ teaspoon finely chopped garlic
1 teaspoon to 1 tablespoon hot red peppers
2 scallions, cut into small pieces

Sauce:

1 tablespoon sherry
2 tablespoons soy sauce
1 tablespoon sweet rice
1 teaspoon sugar
2 tablespoons cornstarch, dissolved in ½ cup water

Preparation

Beat the 2 egg yolks in a medium-sized bowl, add the cut-up chicken, and toss until each piece is well coated. Set aside.

Next, cut up all the vegetables, placing the celery, onion, and red or green pepper on one dish and the scallions, ginger, garlic, and hot red peppers on another. Make the sauce by combining, in a small bowl, the sherry, soy sauce, sweet rice, sugar, and cornstarch-and-water mixture. Set aside.

Cooking

Heat the wok; then add the oil and bring it to a boil. Add the chicken pieces and deep fry them for 5 minutes, stirring occasionally. Add the celery, onion, and peppers and cook for another half minute. Remove the chicken and vegetables from the wok, and drain them well, either on paper towels or in a strainer.

Pour off most of the oil, leaving only about 2 tablespoons for sautéing. Put the remaining vegetables and spices in the wok, and sauté for 1 or 2 minutes. Then add the chicken-and-vegetable mixture and the sauce. Stir well to heat thoroughly. Remove to a serving plate and serve immediately.

Kitchen Favorites and Celebrations
A Chinese meal

The five dishes described on the preceding pages introduce the basic principles of four types of wok cookery: stir-frying, steaming, deep frying and sautéing. The first four recipes were chosen because, when these dishes are served with rice (page 2838), they make an excellent menu for one meal, serving four people. Each has its own unique taste, texture, and color. The fifth dish, made with chicken, could be incorporated into the meal as a substitute for either the beef with broccoli or the steamed fish.

When you plan your own menu, follow these guidelines: the texture of each dish should vary, a main ingredient should not appear twice in the same menu, and the color combination should be attractive. The variation in taste of each dish should also be considered.

If you want to serve a complete Chinese meal, it is better to prepare four average-sized courses than to attempt a large serving of one dish. To do the latter slows the cooking time and changes the character of the dish. Also, having a variety of dishes to sample is enjoyable and closer to authentic serving. This approach requires several woks or other cooking pans, as well as a bit of planning, to make sure each dish is ready to be eaten at one time. For example, since you can serve the Spicy Cabbage at room temperature, prepare it in the morning or the day before. Marinate and steam the duck as long in advance as possible. When you are heating the oil to fry the duck, start the rice. When you turn the duck over to fry the other side, the water for steaming the fish should be boiling. As soon as you have put in the fish to steam, begin to stir-fry the beef with broccoli. With organization like this, everything will be done on time.

Serving

In China, several main dishes are placed in the center of the table so everyone can help himself to a little of each. Rice is always served in small individual bowls at each place. The Chinese use chopsticks instead of forks. Knives are not placed on a Chinese table, since all cutting is done before the food is brought to the table.

Chopsticks

The Chinese are experts with chopsticks and use them as an extension of their fingers to stir, mix, whip, and sort food. Chopsticks vary in length from 5 to 15 inches and are made of silver, ivory, wood, bamboo or even plastic. As shown in photographs 19 through 21, the bottom chopstick remains stationary and the top stick, held much as you would a pencil, acts as a lever to clamp the food. Using chopsticks gracefully takes practice. As your skill increases, you will find that using chopsticks will add to your enjoyment of Chinese food because they add to the authenticity of the meal.

For related entries, see "Hibachi and Hot Pot Cookery."

19: To use chopsticks, hold the upper chopstick firmly between your thumb and the first and second fingers, pencil-fashion.

20: Then position the lower chopstick as shown, resting it on the third finger and at the base of the thumb.

21: Let the lower chopstick remain stationary while you move the upper one up and down so it grips the food.

This wall decoration made of scrap wood, resembling a pair of boxes seen in perspective, won't remain still long enough for the eye to make out what it really is. The illusion is compounded by the artful use of wood grain and by the recessed black borders between pieces. The method of assembly is simple.

WOOD ASSEMBLAGES
Artful Ways with Scraps

Scrap wood accumulated from other projects can be put to good use in abstract modern sculptures for home and garden. Easy to make, such assemblages can be very pleasing to the eye, as attested by their current popularity in museums, galleries, and other public places. Whether made of wood, metal, plastic, or other material, they take their place in a long line of distinguished assemblage crafts—the floor mosaics of Roman masons, the wood-inlay furniture of the Italian renaissance, Indian beadwork, and a host of others. If you work with salvaged lumber that would otherwise be discarded, the cost is next to nothing.

The projects that follow—a wall illusion (opposite), a freestanding abstract sculpture (page 2850), and a trio of heraldic standards (page 2853)—use wood scraps of various sizes. I designed them to make use of my own scraps; you may have to adapt the designs to wood you have on hand, especially in the case of the abstract sculpture project. Or you may prefer to start with new material. Tools and other materials needed are of common household or hardware-store types. The work will go faster if you have power tools, but they are not essential.

Robert Skinner learned wood construction from an old Yankee carpenter many years ago. Since then, he has applied his skills both to creating art works and to building his home. Dr. Skinner is associate professor of fine arts at Southampton College and lives in a geodesic dome in East Hampton, Long Island. His work has been exhibited in many museums and galleries. Most of his raw materials are salvaged from the flotsam of local beaches.

Designs and Decorations
A wall illusion

A simple introductory project in wood assemblage is the box-illusion wall plaque shown opposite. Alternate projects using the same techniques are pictured below; other illusion ideas can be found in psychology and art textbooks. If you develop your own illusion design, be sure it readily confuses the eye before you commit it to wood. I often base such designs on the grain and color of the wood on hand.

Four dynamic illusions made of wood, all really two-dimensional and achieved with the same techniques as the box illusion opposite, blend with the decor of a modern house.

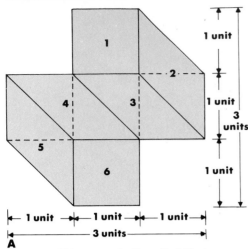

1
2
4 **3**
5
6

1 unit
1 unit
1 unit
3 units
1 unit

1 unit — 1 unit — 1 unit
3 units

A

Figure A: This pattern for the optical-illusion plaque pictured on page 2846 can be enlarged to any size you like; select a scale that will fit your wood scraps. The measurement of each unit in the plaque pictured is 6 inches. The dashed lines—not part of the design—depict the pattern in terms of a grid of squares. However, you only need to enlarge patterns of one parallelogram and one square onto heavy cardboard. But when you have cut out and arranged the six pieces of wood, number the parts as shown.

Materials needed to make the box-illusion wall plaque are: a large sheet of heavy cardboard; four large scraps of wood (one of ½-inch plywood, the others of three contrasting woods of varying thicknesses, if possible); a dozen No. 10 flatheaded wood screws (their length equaling the thickness of the plywood plus half that of the thinnest wood scrap); two ¾-inch No. 10 roundheaded screws; 50-pound-test picture wire; flat black paint; and water-soluble wood putty. Tools required are: pencil; ruler; T square (or carpenter's framing square); scissors; crosscut saw and ripsaw (or saber saw); hand drill (or power drill) with 3/16-inch bit and countersink bit; screwdriver; two C-clamps (or a vise and a clamp); small paintbrush; and 80-grit sandpaper.

To begin, enlarge the design (Figure A) onto heavy cardboard. The size of your pattern will depend on the sizes of the wood scraps you have. In my composition, each unit equals 6 inches. This yields a finished form 18½ inches square (including the small spaces between the pieces). A smaller assemblage would lose impact, but you could make a larger one if you have the material and display space.

Cut out the two basic shapes—a square and a parallelogram—from cardboard. Trace their outlines on the wood scraps to be used in the actual composition—you will need to turn the parallelogram pattern over to get the two mirror images unless the wood is equally good on both sides. It is desirable to use wood of varying thicknesses because this contrast will bring the surfaces into greater relief. Ideally, you would use one kind of wood for the two squares, and cut adjacent pairs of parallelograms from each of the other two kinds of wood. In the wood squares, the grain can run parallel to any edge. But in each parallelogram, the grain should run parallel with a longer side. If you are working with blemished wood, select the side you want to show before you trace the parallelogram.

To avoid confusion during assembly, lightly number the wood shapes with a pencil as shown in Figure A. Using a crosscut saw (across the grain) or a ripsaw (with the grain), cut out all six wooden shapes.

The Base
These shapes will be mounted on a shaped base that must be large enough to permit ¼ inch of space between the pieces. This small gap makes them stand out more effectively. Using ½-inch plywood as this base, arrange the shapes on it by number, starting in a square corner. Insert ¼-inch-thick spacers between the pieces; then trace the overall shape on the base (photograph 1). If you are working in a much smaller or larger scale than 6 inches per unit, alter the width of the spacers proportionately. Remove the shapes and spacers, and check right angles within the outline for accuracy, using a framing square or T square (photograph 2). Saw the baseboard shape from the plywood (photograph 3).

Place the shapes and spacers back on the base so you can outline each shape, removing spacers as necessary to let the pencil pass but holding the shapes firmly in place (photograph 4). Outer edges of the shapes should be flush with the edges of the base. Sand all edges of the shapes and base with 80-grit sandpaper, and fill any cracks or splits with water-soluble putty. Let it dry; then resand as necessary. (Do not sand away the reference numbers yet.) paint the edges of the base, as well as the spaces between the paired pencil outlines on the base, with flat black paint. The edges of the shapes are not painted.

Let the paint dry; then mark the paint-outlined sections of the base for the screws that will hold the shapes in place (photograph 5). Allow two screws for each shape, 1 or 2 inches in from opposite corners. Use a 3/16-inch bit to drill all twelve screw holes. Bore completely through the base starting from the top (photograph 6). Turn the base over and countersink the holes so the flatheaded screws can be driven flush with the surface (photograph 7).

Turn the base face up. Working with one of the shapes at a time, clamp it to the base, using a scrap of wood to keep the clamp from marring the shape. If you let the base extend beyond the edge of your workbench, you can screw the shape in place from below (photograph 8). Clamp the rest of the base to the workbench. Drive No. 10 flatheaded wood screws through the pilot holes and into the shapes. The screws should be long enough so they penetrate halfway into the shapes. If the shapes are hardwood, you will need to drill pilot holes in them before driving the screws. Drive screws into the remaining shapes in the same way.

1: To mark a plywood base for the box illusion, lay out the shapes according to the number sequence in Figure A. All pieces are lying flat. Insert ¼-inch spacers between the shapes, and trace the overall outline on the plywood.

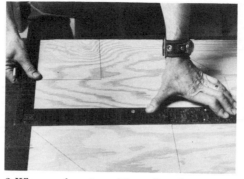

2: When you have traced the outline, clear the plywood. Using a framing square or T square, check the accuracy of the right angles. If you have a 45-degree drafting triangle, you can also check the diagonal lines.

3: Saw the outlined shape from the plywood scrap. To minimize fraying of the plywood edges, saw with an even, rhythmic motion, applying light pressure on the downstroke, and avoid contact on the backstroke.

4: Return the wood shapes and spacers to the plywood while you trace the outline of each shape. When you remove a spacer to let the pencil pass, hold the adjacent shapes immobile with your fingers. Tracing each piece will give you a double line between pieces.

5: Paint the edges of the base and the strips that will show between shapes, using flat black paint. (Stray paint will be concealed by the shapes.) Then mark the locations for two screw holes on each of the six sections, 1 or 2 inches in from opposite corners.

6: Using a 3/16-inch drill bit (for No. 10 screws), bore all 12 holes through the plywood. Center them on the points previously marked. Keep the painted side up, so the fraying that takes place when the drill bit emerges from the plywood will occur on the back face of the base.

7: Change to a countersink bit, turn the plywood over, and widen the holes so flat screw heads can be driven flush with the surface. If screw heads protrude, the plaque will not hang flat on a wall.

8: One at a time, clamp the shapes to the base and clamp the base to the workbench, so you drive screws from below. If the screws do not enter the shapes easily, drill pilot holes for them.

9: To hang the assemblage, drive screws at opposite sides of the back of the base, 1 inch below the top of the middle third. Bridge them with taut heavy-duty picture wire.

I have experimented with using glue to secure the shapes to the baseboard, but I have found it unsatisfactory, especially if old wood is used. Too, I prefer leaving the wood shapes in their natural state, without a finish. The only finishing touch necessary is to sand the face of the shapes lightly to erase the pencil marks.

Select whatever orientation of the illusion you like best—it works equally well when viewed from any direction. For hanging, drive two ¾-inch No. 10 round-headed screws halfway into the back of the base, 1 inch in from each side and ½ inch below the top of the middle third. Span the screws with 50-pound-test picture wire (photograph 9). Use a heavy picture hook if you hang the plaque on a plaster wall.

10: To make the freestanding wood sculpture, cut the boards to the desired length; then enlarge the pattern (Figure B) onto the wood.

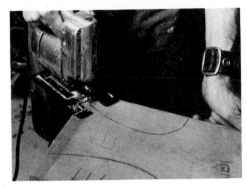

11: Use a saber saw or a coping saw to cut away those sections of wood outside of the curved pattern lines.

Designs and Decorations
A freestanding sculpture

Large assemblages, like the freestanding sculpture shown below, pose interesting challenges. Clever joinery techniques are often needed to solve problems of physical as well as artistic balance. And the question of a proper setting, whether indoors or out, must be considered.

This wood sculpture was made from two 14-foot lengths of 2-by-12-inch fir, salvaged from the ruins of an abandoned building. (I have found similar planks in the surf and at construction dumps.) The exact dimensions of the wood are unimportant; if you try this project, you can adapt the dimensions to whatever wood you have. The quality of the scrap is also unimportant because the plan can be adjusted to permit the removal of knots and other flaws. You also need 4 feet of ½-inch dowel (also called ½-inch round); a few scrap 2-by-4s; waterproof white glue; and, in addition to the tools listed on page 2848, a coping saw; two bar clamps; a ½-inch drill bit; and four sawhorses. I used power tools, but the work could easily be done without them.

A freestanding abstract sculpture, made from two wood planks in a few hours, seems at home in this woodland setting. The cat likes it too.

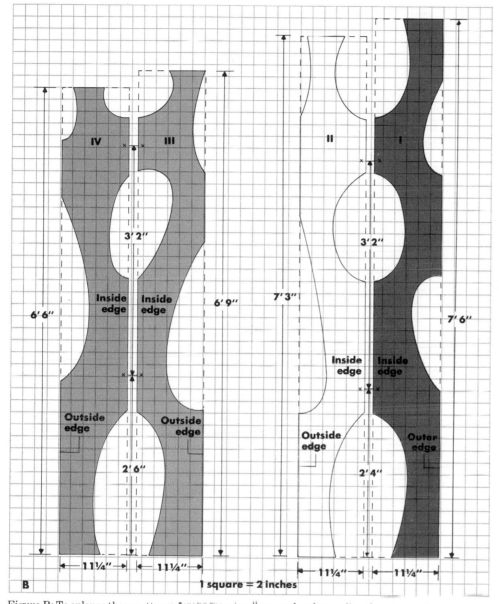

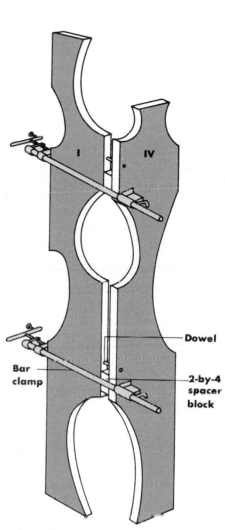

Figure B: To enlarge these patterns for the freestanding wood sculpture directly onto your lumber, draw a 2-inch grid on each piece of wood. Reproduce the curves by copying the pattern, square by square. You can draw horizontal grid lines quickly by placing all four boards side by side and flush at the bottom, marking the outer edge of the outer boards at 2-inch intervals, and connecting the marked points. To draw vertical lines quickly, set a combination square to the length required (2 inches, then 4 inches, and so forth), and run it along the board's edge while you hold a pencil at the end of its arm. The Xs in the figure mark the centers of dowel holes.

Figure C: Join sections of the wood sculpture at right angles by clamping them together with 2-by-4 spacer blocks between, then drilling holes and gluing dowels in them. The spacer blocks will be removed later.

Begin by removing nails and large splinters from the planks and scraping or sanding the surface. (If you are working with weathered driftwood, you may want to omit the latter step.) Measure and saw a 7½-foot length from one plank, leaving a 6½-foot piece. Cut the other plank into 7-foot, 3-inch and 6-foot, 9-inch segments. Place the four boards on the floor and label them I, II, III, and IV in order of decreasing length. Then transfer the patterns to the boards (Figure B and photograph 10). If your boards are of a different size or have flaws that need to be cut away, adapt the pattern to suit them. Cut out the boards along the curving lines, using a coping saw or saber saw (photograph 11). Then sand all the edges smooth.

Begin the assembly by preparing to join boards I and IV (the longest and the shortest). Stand them at right angles to each other, and clamp them together as shown in Figure C, with the inside edge of board IV overlapping the inside edge of board I, and with two short 2-by-4-inch blocks inserted between them. (Inside and outside edges are labeled in Figure B). Check the right angle with a framing

12: After you have clamped a pair of boards together (Figure C), drill ½-inch holes 5 inches deep at the points marked X in Figure B, through the top board, past the separator block, and into the edge of the second board.

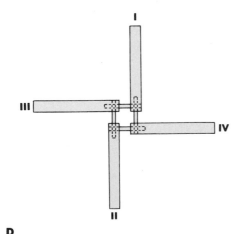

13: For outdoor display, use polyurethane paint to color the finished assembly in a variety of bright and glossy hues. First paint the least accessible areas—the edges and dowels.

D

Figure D: A bird's-eye view of the assembled wood sculpture shows how the four boards are lapped and joined by dowels.

square; if it is off by a few degrees, tighten or loosen the clamps to correct it. Mark centers for two dowel holes on board IV, ¾ inch in from the joining edge at heights of 30 and 68 inches from the bottom. These are marked X in Figure B. Carefully place the clamped boards across a pair of sawhorses. Use a ½-inch bit to drill holes at the marked points (photograph 12). Drill through board IV, past the separator blocks and into the edge of board I, as far as the drill bit permits (or 5 inches in all). Be careful to drill straight; the thickness of board I leaves little room for error. Cut two lengths of dowel slightly shorter than the combined hole-spacer-hole depth. Test for fit; then coat both pairs of holes with waterproof white glue. Tap in the dowels until they are flush with the surface of board IV (Figure D). After the glue has dried (allow about an hour), remove the clamps and assemble boards II and III in the same way. Clamp them together with the inside edge of board III overlapping the inside edge of board II. Insert dowels at the same height as before.

When the glue has hardened, stand both pairs of boards upright, and clamp boards II and IV together (using separator blocks as before) with board II overlapping board IV (Figures C, page 2851, and D). If you have a second pair of bar clamps, join boards I and III at the same time, with board I overlapping board III. Otherwise this can be done in a second sequence. To join the two halves of the assemblage, place the clamped boards between two pairs of sawhorses, with board II pointing down and boards III and IV resting on the sawhorses. Since board III is higher than board IV, prop it up on 3-inch scraps to forestall wobbling. Mark board I and board II for dowel holes ¾ inch in from the inner edge and, this time, at heights of 28 and 66 inches from the bottom to avoid the dowels already in place. Bore holes through board II and into the edge of board IV; then insert dowels as before. Finally, do the same to join board I to board III.

The finished assemblage can be stained, painted, or—in the case of seasoned or weathered wood—left natural. If the sculpture is to be displayed outdoors, use a primer and a coat of polyurethane paint (photograph 13). For best results, paint all the board edges and dowels first because they are the hardest parts to reach. Painting them white makes the boards stand out from each other. Then paint the board faces in any colors you like; color will cover any stray white paint.

Designs and Decorations
Abstract heraldic standards

In medieval times, armies marching into battle carried colorful insignia for identification, borne aloft on poles. A modern adaptation of this idea is the trio of heraldic standards pictured opposite. Bright and decorative, this composition of scrap wood adds a cheerful note to playroom or patio.

To make it, you will need: a 6½-foot length of 2-by-12-inch lumber (or its equivalent in smaller scraps); three pieces of ½-inch round hardwood (or plumbing pipe) 6½, 7, and 8 feet long; masking tape; all-purpose white glue; a railroad tie or similar heavy beam about 4 feet long; 2½ dozen No. 10 flatheaded wood screws, ¾ inch in length (or, for pipe, 3/16-by-1-inch flatheaded stove bolts); and flat black paint, primer, and marine paints in assorted colors. In addition to the tools listed on pages 2848 and 2850, you will need: a drawing compass; 1/16-inch, ⅝-inch, and 5/32-inch drill bits; a round wood rasp; and No. 120 garnet abrasive paper. You can adapt the instructions that follow to use materials on hand.

Draw the pattern shown in Figure E on the 6½-foot board. If you are working with shorter scraps, you can break the pattern into any of the five sections indicated by red lines in the diagram. (The black areas represent waste—less than 5 percent.) The curved lines are segments of a circle; all can be drawn with a compass following the radius dimensions given. Number all the shapes lightly with a pencil as indicated. The dashed lines, which do not represent saw cuts, should also be marked for reference when mounting holes are drilled.

With a crosscut or saber saw, cut the board or scraps at the red lines into sections (photograph 14). Then cut along the remaining solid lines, using a coping saw or saber saw to make curved cuts. Start internal circular cuts by drilling a 1/16-inch hole through any point on the circumference (photograph 15), then passing either coping or saber saw blade through the hole (photograph 16).

A few geometric forms cut from scrap lumber, fastened to poles and painted bright colors, make contemporary heraldic standards.

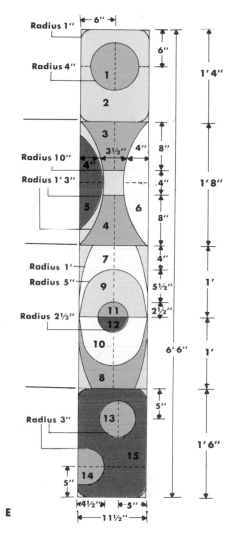

E

Figure E: The pattern for the abstract wooden shapes on the three heraldic standards shows how all 15 pieces can be cut from a single 12-inch board 6½ feet long. To transfer this pattern to the wood, draft it mechanically, following the dimensions given. Number all parts. Use a crosscut saw to divide the board into manageable sections, marked by red lines. Do not cut along the dashed lines which locate holes to be drilled. The black areas are waste.

14: Using a crosscut saw, cut the wood into the easy-to-handle sections marked in Figure E with red lines.

15: To start an internal curving saw cut, drill a 1/16-inch hole any place on the perimeter of the shape that is to be removed.

16: Once the hole is drilled, insert the blade of a coping or saber saw and make the cut. (A coping saw must be assembled in place.)

17: Extend the dashed lines of the pattern onto the adjoining edges of the pieces, with a combination square and pencil. Then use the square's rule to locate the midpoint along each of the edges for centering your drill bit.

18: Clamp each shape to a bench leg, with one edge flat on the floor or on scrap wood. Drill straight down into the top edge, all the way through. If the bit is not long enough, reverse the piece and drill from the other edge.

19: With a long, round wood rasp, you can adjust any holes that are slightly off center because you drilled in two directions to a central meeting point. You have a ⅛-inch margin of error, since the pieces do not fit snugly on the poles.

20: Assemble the shapes on the poles, with backs facing up, and drill two 5/32-inch holes through each piece and into the pole. Center the screw holes 1 inch in from the top and bottom edges.

21: Paint the shapes; then fasten them to the poles with screws, using the drilled holes. If you use a pipe for the pole, attach the pieces with stove bolts, driven partway through the pipe.

To prepare to drill holes for mounting the shapes on poles, use a square to extend the dashed lines (Figure E, page 2853) across the adjacent edges of each piece. Then, with pencil and combination square, mark the midpoint of these new lines (photograph 17). One at a time, clamp the pieces, with the marked edge on top, onto a workbench leg, setting the lower edge flat on the floor. Using a ⅝-inch bit and holding the drill vertical (check with a framing square), bore down into the top edge of the piece until the tip of the bit emerges from the bottom edge (photograph 18). If you do not want to mar the floor, put a scrap of wood between it and the workpiece. With the pieces numbered 1, 3, 4, 9, 10, 13, and 15, your drill bit will probably be too short to reach the opposite edge. If so, either use an extension bit or invert the workpiece and bore from the opposite end until the two holes meet. This requires care but there is some leeway—about ⅛ inch—for error. If the holes are slightly out of alignment, you can clamp the board in a vise and correct the error with a long, round wood rasp (photograph 19).

Laying one pole at a time across the workbench, slip the shapes onto the pole in sequence with their backs facing up. Position them at the heights indicated in Figure F. As the shapes will fit loosely, mark the location of each on the pole.

With a 5/32-inch bit, drill two holes through each shape and into the pole, centering a hole 1 inch inside the top and the bottom edge of the shape (photograph 20). To ensure the proper depth, mark your drill bit with masking tape ¾ inch from the tip. Finally, countersink the holes in the numbered shapes. (If you use plumbing pipe, drill only as far as the pipe—thus marking it with your bit. Remove the wooden shapes, secure the pipe in a vise, and complete the holes through one side of the pipe.)

File away any rough edges on the shapes and smooth all surfaces with 80-grit sandpaper. Paint the shapes with white undercoat. When they are dry, sand them lightly with No. 120 garnet paper. Give each shape two finishing coats of glossy marine paint, using a variety of bright colors. When the paint is dry, reassemble

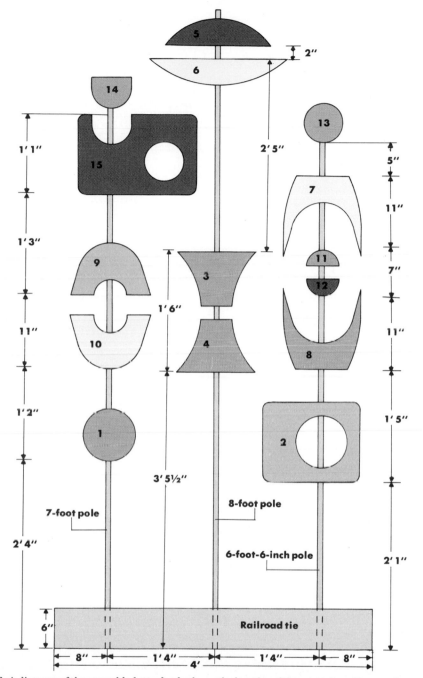

F

Figure F: A diagram of the assembled standards shows the location of the parts, keyed by number to Figure E, as well as the heavy base that supports and integrates the construction.

the pieces on the poles, and set them with their backs facing up on a clean surface. Attach them to the poles with ¾-inch No. 10 flatheaded screws (photograph 21). If the poles are metal, use 3/16-by-1-inch flatheaded stove bolts. After protecting the tops and bottoms of all the shapes with masking tape, paint the exposed areas of the pole with flat black paint. When it is dry, remove the masking tape.

An ideal support for the poles is a 4-foot length of railroad tie or other wood beam at least 6 by 6 inches. (You can make such a beam by nailing thinner boards to-gether.) Drill three ⅝-inch holes in the support, each 5 inches deep. Space them 16 inches apart and center them with respect to the width and length of the support. If the poles fit too loosely, they may be wedged into the holes with small nails. Paint the support with flat black paint.

For related projects and crafts, see "Collages and Assemblages," "Sculpture," and "Yard Toys."

WOVEN TAPESTRIES
Pictures on a Loom

The word tapestry usually brings to mind the magnificent French and Flemish wall-sized hangings created during the Middle Ages, works like the famous unicorn tapestries. But tapestries predate the Middle Ages by thousands of years. The word goes back to the ancient Greek *tapès*, meaning carpet, and these textiles appeared in ancient Greece, Rome, and Egypt. Tapestries have varied in style and use from culture to culture and time to time, as has the meaning of the word. At first the term meant a heavy, woven textile, usually pictorial, that was used as a decorative covering for a floor or wall. Occasionally, tapestry-style weavings were used on windows and furniture; some were even incorporated into garments. In time the definition became vague until almost any fabric floor or wall covering could be called a tapestry. For example, the famous Bayeux tapestry, made in the eleventh century, is actually embroidery stitched on a plain woven background.

Swedish-born Anita Askild (left) divides her time among painting, weaving, and textile designing. Her extensive art training began in her native country, and continued at the Art Students' League when she moved to New York. Her weaving skills, however, are largely self-taught; her love for tapestries evolved from the close relationship tapestry weaving bears to painting. Many of her works are in private collections.

Josè Amadeo-Holl (right) attended the University of Massachusetts in Amherst. He enjoys making furniture and is particularly proud of a tapestry loom, pictured opposite, that he designed and made for Anita Askild. Directions for making a simplified version of this loom begin on page 2864.

Tapestries have a long history, and each culture has its own traditional designs, colors, yarns, and uses. The Navaho Indian who made this blanket used handspun, natural-dyed wool.

Opposite: Anita Askild is pictured weaving a tapestry on her hand-built loom. Her cat is as unusual as his name, Robin Hood, in that he has no interest whatsoever in playing with balls of yarn.

Glossary of tapestry-weaving terms

Beating: Tamping down each crosswise (weft) thread after it has been passed over and under lengthwise (warp) threads, to make the weave firm. In a tapestry, the weft is usually beaten so tightly that the warp is completely covered.

Butterfly: Thread or yarn wound in a figure-eight configuration so it can be passed back and forth through the warp without getting tangled.

Cartoon: A full-sized pattern of the design used as a guide during weaving.

Heddles: A series of string loops attached to a rod, through which alternate warp threads are passed.

Heddle rod: The bar on a loom that holds string loops (heddles).

Loom: A device on which warp threads are put to keep them under even tension while they are woven with weft threads.

Selvages: The side edges of a weaving.

Shed: The open space between two layers of warp threads, through which the weft thread is passed. A shed is created when every other warp thread is raised with fingers, a shed stick, or string loops (heddles).

Shed stick: A thin stick, usually made of hardwood, used to lift a layer of alternate warp threads as a unit so the weft thread can be passed through easily.

Warp: Lengthwise threads that are strung on the loom, through which the crosswise threads (weft) are woven.

Weft: The crosswise threads that are woven through the warp threads on a loom. The weft is also called the filling.

Because tapestries require many color changes within rows, they are usually worked with the wrong side facing the weaver. This facilitates joining the colors. To prevent tangles, the yarns used are wound into small bundles, called butterflies, which are left dangling when not in use.

The Tapestry Weave

The weaving technique used in making modern tapestries is one of the easiest to learn. These tapestries consist of stationary lengthwise threads (called the warp) interlaced with crosswise threads (called the weft). What makes it easy is that only one weaving pattern is used—the plain weave—in which each weft thread goes over one warp thread and under the next. Tapestry weaving differs from other types of weaving in that the rows of weft threads usually do not travel entirely across the warp, from one edge to the other. Instead, the weft is woven in small sections dictated by the shapes and colors of the design, as pictured above. This allows great freedom in the intricacy or boldness of the design you can create and in the number of colors you can use. The weft is usually packed down (beaten) so tightly that no warp is visible. This gives a tapestry its characteristically ribbed surface.

Looms

Tapestries are woven on a loom. It keeps the lengthwise (warp) threads that are stretched on it under tension so the crosswise threads (weft) can be woven through easily. Tapestry weaving can be done on any type of loom, from the simplest to the most complex. Although I sometimes use a special tapestry loom (page 2856), a frame loom can also be used. Instructions for making two types of frame looms are given on these pages, and all of the projects that follow can be woven on either one. The simple frame loom (page 2861) is easily and inexpensively made and is portable. On page 2864 is a somewhat more complex frame loom, designed especially for tapestry weaving. While this loom is harder to build, it lets certain steps in the weaving go more quickly. How each loom works is described following the construction details.

Yarn

When you choose a warp yarn, bear in mind that it will be under tension on the loom. For strength, linen or cotton is often used. You can also use ordinary wrapping twine and string (available in hardware and variety stores) or rug warp (available in weaving-supply shops). If a yarn is not marked for use as warp, test its strength by trying to break it with your hands. If it breaks easily, don't use it.

Another consideration in choosing yarn is the color of the warp. In traditional tapestry weaving, since the warp is hidden by the weft, white, off-white, or beige

Almost any yarn can be used as weft for weaving tapestries. Pictured above are (top row, left to right): rug wool, two skeins of rya yarn, Swedish weaving yarn, Donegal tweed knitting or weaving wool, heavy hand-spun wool, gold metallic thread, decorative braid used as trim in sewing; (bottom row, left to right): crochet cotton (also used as warp), rayon boucle yarn, jute, two skeins of raffia, knitting worsted, cotton embroidery floss, crochet cotton in two weights, hand-spun, natural-dyed wool with embroidery silk below it.

Tapestry-weaving supplies
Before you order supplies, request a catalogue from any of the following mail-order suppliers:

Coulter Studios
118 East 59th Street
New York, N. Y. 10022
(Tapestry looms and weaving yarns)

Craft Yarns of Rhode Island Inc.
P. O. Box 151
Harrisville, R. I. 02830
(Weaving yarns)

The Niddy Noddy
416 Albany Post Road
Croton-on-Hudson, N. Y. 10520
(Looms and weaving yarns)

Schacht Spindle Co.
1708 Walnut Street
Boulder, Colo. 80302
(Tapestry looms)

School Products Co.
1201 Broadway
New York, N. Y. 10001
(Tapestry looms)

The Yarn Depot
545 Sutter Street
San Francisco, Calif. 94102
(Weaving yarns)

warp is used. If you like to experiment, you can leave the warp exposed in some areas, but this means choosing the warp color in relation to the weft colors.

In choosing weft yarns, on the other hand, you have complete freedom. There is no reason to use only yarns designated for weaving or tapestry work. I use anything that strikes my fancy, from metallic threads and fine silk to the bulky synthetic yarns sold in variety stores. Since the work is done in small sections, you can incorporate short lengths of yarn left over from previous projects, including weaving yarns, embroidery floss, knitting yarns, and crocheting thread. Just avoid changing during the weaving process from a thin, lightweight yarn to a heavy one. Such a change may make the surface buckle.

Preliminaries

Before you start weaving, make a full-sized sketch of the design you plan to weave. Called a cartoon, this drawing is essential. Keep the cartoon at hand for reference. If it is convenient, put it behind the warp and tape it to the frame you are weaving on. Or transfer the outlines of the design onto the warp threads, using paint or felt-tipped pens, either working freehand or using the cartoon underneath as a guide.

As another preliminary, decide the direction you will weave. Tapestries are usually planned as wall hangings, and they are traditionally woven from end to end, sideways, across the tapestry length. This is done because the weft (horizontal threads on the loom) is more tightly packed than the warp and hence is more supportive. If the design is so arranged that the weft threads run vertically when the tapestry is hung, it helps prevent sagging. Most tapestries are not so large that sagging is a problem, but the number of color joinings, and the easiest way to achieve them, is a concern in making any tapestry. If the design, when upright, contains long vertical shapes or lines of unbroken color, weave from end to end on the loom. That way, the long elements will be continuous across the warp instead of being assembled vertically. The wall hanging on page 2870 was woven sideways for this reason.

Just as tapestry weaving is usually done from end to end, it is often worked with the wrong side facing the weaver. This permits neater joinings (Craftnotes, pages 2868 and 2869). The patterns for the three projects that follow are all shown in reverse. You can weave a tapestry right side up if you feel that gives you more control, but the design that results will be a mirror image of the one pictured.

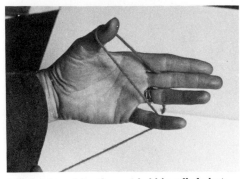 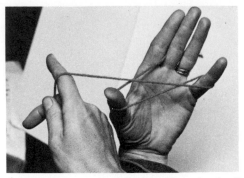

1: To begin making the yarn bobbin called a butterfly, anchor the yarn between your first and second fingers, pass it around your thumb from the outside, then take it around your little finger.

2: Bring the yarn across the palm of your hand so it crosses itself. Then wrap it around the inside of your thumb again, forming a figure eight which keeps the yarn tangle free.

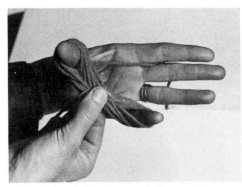 

3: Continue winding the yarn in figure eights, back and forth around thumb and little finger. Lift the butterfly from your hand by grasping the yarn where it crosses in the middle.

4: To secure the butterfly, transfer it to the other hand and wrap the free end of the yarn around the middle. Do not wrap too tightly or the yarn will not release freely later.

5: Pull the free end through the last wrapping, forming a loop that you pull tight. The end coming from the inside of the yarn butterfly is the one you pull to release the yarn as you weave.

Finally, prepare butterfly bobbins of the weft yarns you will be using (photographs 1 through 5). Putting yarn into bundles in this fashion makes it easier to carry lengths of weft back and forth through the warp. If the area you are weaving in a certain color is small, you can forgo making a butterfly and work with a short piece of yarn, using it as is or threaded through a tapestry needle.

Weaving, Braiding, and Knotting
Simple frame loom

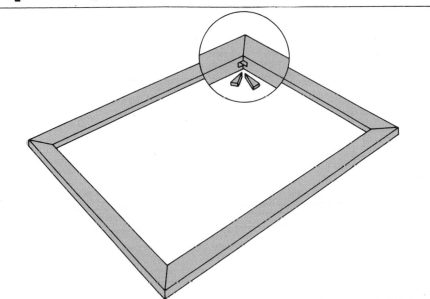

A

Figure A: To make a simple frame loom using artist's canvas stretcher strips, assemble the strips by interlocking the corners. Then insert the wedge-shaped wooden pegs for stability by pounding them into the inner corners of the frame with a hammer.

To make a simple frame loom, you need four canvas-stretcher strips (sold in pairs at art supply stores) or any other smooth 1-by-2-inch wood strips. The size of the frame will be determined by the size of the tapestry you want to weave. Many weavers have several frames, each sized to a tapestry they plan to weave. However, you can use one loom for many weavings. One that is 3 feet square will be adequate for all the projects shown here and can be built without corner braces or other extra supports. If you make a loom of a different size it should be at least 8 inches longer and 6 inches wider than the biggest tapestry you plan to make. This gives you room to manipulate the weft through the warp. If you build a frame larger than 3 feet square, use thicker wood and add corner braces for rigidity. I do not recommend a frame loom larger than 6 feet square.

Assemble the wood strips to form a rectangle, making sure the corners form right angles. If you use stretcher strips, interlock the mitered corners using the wooden pegs that come with the strips (Figure A). For additional corner strength, use staples or wood screws to anchor the joints. If you use lumber other than stretcher strips, sand all edges smooth. Lay the two shorter strips on top of the two longer strips, forming a rectangle. Make sure the corners are square; then clamp the wood securely and drill two pilot holes in each corner. Drill through the top strip of wood and halfway through the bottom strip. Insert wood screws long enough to go well into the bottom strips.

Warping the Loom.

The next step is to stretch the warp threads on the loom. On a frame loom, the warp is one continuous strand wrapped around the top and bottom strips. Using a pencil and ruler, mark the planned width of the weaving on the outer edges of the top and bottom strips, centering it between the sides. To space the warp evenly, divide the marked area into inches, and then each inch into the number of wrappings per inch required. For most tapestries, four marks per inch is the norm; this results in eight warps per inch (four front and four back). Before you wrap the yarn around the loom, you can draw a wood saw lightly across each mark to make a narrow notch in the wood (sand the wood lightly after you do this). These notches will keep the warp threads in place. If you do not notch the wood, chain the warp threads as described on page 2862 after you complete the warping.

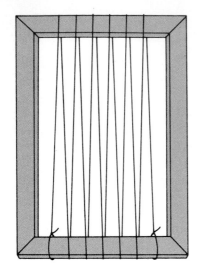

B

Figure B: To put the warp on a frame loom, knot one end of the yarn to the bottom left corner of the frame, placing it at the first pencil mark or in the first notch. Then start winding the yarn in a figure eight, taking it over the front of the top strip (at the first mark or notch on top), then down and over the front of the bottom strip (at the second mark or notch on the bottom), around and back up again. Continue winding the yarn, placing the thread at successive marks or notches. Fasten the warp by tying it to the bottom strip at the end. (For clarity, only a few warp threads are shown; commonly there are eight to the inch, four on top and four on the bottom.)

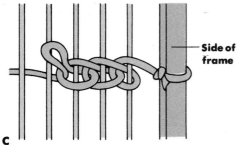

C

Figure C: To begin chaining warp threads, tie one end of a strong cord to the right side of the frame. With your left hand, hold it taut behind the warp. Place the thumb and forefinger of your right hand under the cord at the right edge of the loom, and pull the cord up, forming a loop that you lay over the first warp thread. With your fingers still in the first loop, reach down between the first and second warp and pick up additional cord. Loop it through the loop you just formed. With thumb and forefinger inserted in the second loop, reach down between the second and third warps and pick up another loop. Continue picking up and pulling loops between adjacent warps until each warp thread is in a loop. Pull each loop snugly into position as soon as it is locked with a new loop, so the finished loops are tight and evenly spaced.

Side of frame

6: To pass the weft through the first shed on a simple frame loom, put your hand through the opening between the layers and pull the butterfly through.

7: To form the second shed on a frame loom, pull up the lower layer of warp threads, one by one, with your index finger. Start near the side where the first row of weaving ended.

8: After you have picked up the number of warp threads required by the area of the design, put your thumb under them as well so you can grasp the butterfly.

9: Holding the butterfly in your right hand, pull it through the shed you have made. If you will weave across the entire row, continue lifting groups of warps all the way across.

To warp the loom, tie the end of the warp yarn around the bottom stretcher strip, placing the yarn at the left mark or notch. Wind the yarn around the frame in a figure eight, keeping it taut (Figure B).

If you have not notched the frame, make a row of chaining across the bottom of the warp before you begin to weave. This serves two purposes: it spaces the warp evenly and it provides a sturdy foundation against which you can beat the first few rows of weft. Tie one end of a strong cord around the right side of the frame, close to the bottom. To form the chain, make a loop around each warp thread as shown in Figure C. To finish, pass the free end of the cord through the last loop on the left side of the warp, and tie the end to the left side of the frame.

Weaving

Tapestry weaving is based on a plain weave in which the weft threads pass over and under alternate warp threads. For one row of weaving, all the odd-numbered threads are lifted and the weft passes under them; for the next row, all the even-numbered threads are lifted. Lifting is accomplished by various means, depending on the type of loom you use. Each time a set of threads is lifted, you form what is called a shed. By repeating the process of lifting a set of threads to form a shed, passing the weft through the shed, and beating it down into position, you are weaving.

On a frame loom, the thickness of the frame and the figure-eight configuration of the warp keeps alternate warp strands separated into a top and bottom layer. This forms the first shed. Use it to begin the weaving. Hold the end of the butterfly yarn at the right side of the loom as you pull the butterfly through the shed (photograph 6). To form the second shed (called a counter shed), lift up the bottom threads so they are on top (photograph 7). Then pass the weft back through this second shed (photographs 8 and 9). The weft now passes over the warp threads it passed under in the first shed, and under those it passed over, locking the weave in place.

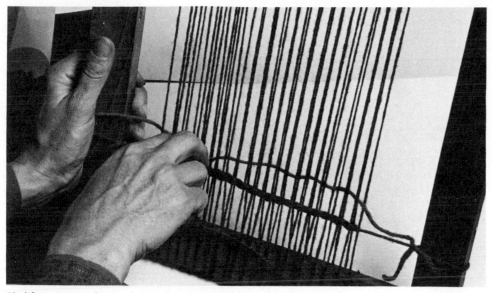

10: After you complete each row of weaving, beat the weft yarn down into place. You can use a hair comb or table fork for this, but fingers work quite well.

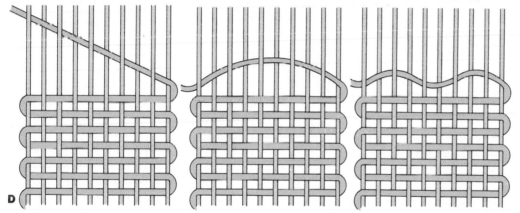

Figure D: To prevent the warp threads from being pulled in at the sides, which would make the weaving progressively narrower, lay the weft in loosely. This can be accomplished by slanting it (left), arching it (center), or bubbling it (right).

After you weave each row, close the shed by letting the warp return to its original position. Then beat the weft down in place, using your fingers, a comb, or a table fork (photograph 10). To beat, tap down gently but firmly until no warp is visible between the rows of weft.

On pages 2868 and 2869, you will find Craftnotes that show many ways you can join adjacent sections of your tapestry. To begin and end each section, leave a short tail of weft yarn dangling on the wrong side of the tapestry. Since the weft is tightly packed, the yarn will stay in place without unraveling. In tapestry weaving, unlike other forms of weaving, you can leave an unkempt back (tapestries that have many color changes often look like shaggy rugs).

The sides (selvages) of the tapestry should be uniform throughout. Because you will be weaving shapes in sections and using various weights of yarn, the tapestry will tend to grow narrower as the weaving progresses. To forestall this, always take the weft through the shed loosely enough so it covers the warp without pulling on the selvages after it is tamped down. Figure D shows three ways to do this. In addition, periodically pass a length of strong cord around the end warps, pull the weaving to its proper width, then tie the cords to the sides of the loom. When you have finished weaving, make a second row of chaining at the top of the tapestry. Remove it from the frame by cutting the warp threads at the top and bottom. Warp by warp, unravel the chaining, tying each adjacent pair of warp ends together with an overhand knot as they are freed (Figure E).

Figure E: Use simple overhand knots to tie pairs of adjacent warp ends together, close to the last row of weaving. This keeps the weaving from unraveling.

Tapestry frame loom

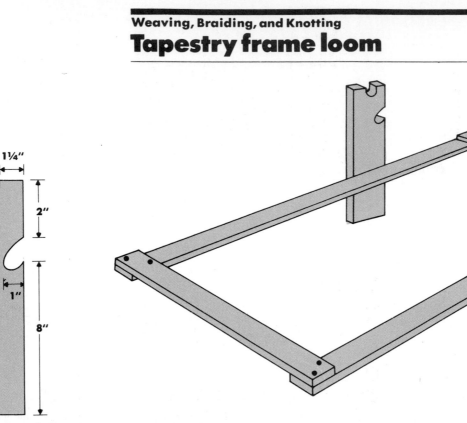

1¼" 1¼"

2"

1"

8"

F

Figure F: These measurements indicate the positions of grooves needed in heddle-rod supports.

8"

4½"

G

Figure G: Use wood screws to attach each heddle-rod support to a side of the frame. Place each support 8 inches away from the top edge of the frame, and raise the frame so it is 4½ inches above the bottom of the support. When you measure and mark this position, lift only the top edge of the frame.

José Holl's tapestry loom, shown on page 2856, is an intricate structure. A simplified version that operates in a similar manner is shown in Figure F. The basic construction is similar to that of the simple frame loom, and you can build the frame by following the directions on page 2861. After you have assembled the frame, reinforce the corners and use sandpaper to smooth any rough edges that might catch the yarn.

This loom differs from the first in two respects. First, a stick is used to form the odd-numbered sheds. Even-numbered sheds are created by lifting string heddles attached to the warp threads so the weaver does not need to pick up individual warp threads with each pass of the weft.

Making and Warping the Loom

To make the shed stick, you need a piece of hardwood, short enough to fit inside the frame but 3 to 4 inches longer than the width of the tapestry. It should be ⅜ inch thick and about 1½ inches wide. Using sandpaper, round and smooth the edges of the stick. Sharp edges would cut the warp.

The warp threads are lifted as units by loops of string, called heddles, connected to a bar called a heddle rod. For the heddle rod, use a wooden dowel ¾ inch in diameter; the length should be the width of the loom plus 3 inches. To make supports for the heddle rod, use 11-inch lengths of 1-by-4-inch lumber. With pencil and ruler, mark the position of the grooves (Figure F). Clamp a support so it cannot shift, and use a coping saw to cut the grooves. Then use a round or half-round wood file to smooth the edges. Finally, sand each piece of wood smooth.

Use wood screws to attach the heddle-rod supports to the loom, as shown in Figure G, drilling pilot holes first. When attached, these supports provide two places to rest the heddle rod and lift the top of the loom, making the process of weaving more comfortable.

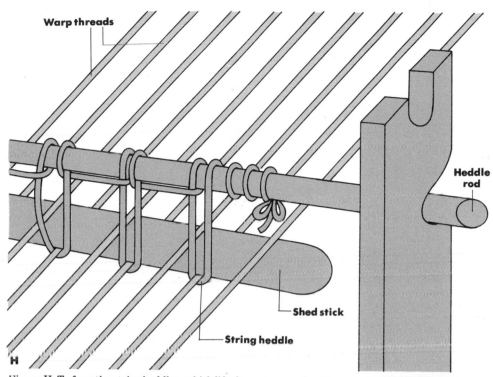

Warp threads

Heddle rod

Shed stick

String heddle

H

11: To form the first shed on the tapestry-frame loom, turn the shed stick on edge. Then pass the weft yarn through.

Figure H: To form the string heddles, which lift alternate warp threads as a unit, tie a length of string to the right end of the heddle rod. Wrap the string around the rod until you reach the second warp thread (the first thread under the shed stick). Pass the string under this warp, bring it up to the rod, around it, and then through the loop thus formed. Make a spacer loop in the same way, without passing the string under a warp. Make a heddle for the next warp that is under the shed stick, make a spacer loop, and so on, until all the warps under the shed stick have heddles. Wrap the string around the rod a few times and knot it. (Widely spaced warp threads are shown for clarity.)

To warp the loom, wrap the lengthwise thread around the top and bottom strips, following the directions for warping the simple frame loom (page 2861).

To make string heddles, rest the heddle rod in the back (lower) grooves of the supports. At the top of the loom, put the shed stick through the warp, separating the top and bottom layers of yarn. Move the stick down so it is directly under the heddle rod. Wind a 2-yard length of cotton or linen string or thread into a butterfly (you can use the same yarn you used for the warp). Tie the end of the butterfly to the right side of the heddle rod, about ½ inch from the first warp thread. Then form heddles connecting the lower layer of warp threads to the heddle rod, as shown in Figure H.

12: For the second shed, grasp a number of heddles and pull them toward you, thus lifting the lower warp threads. Then pass the weft through.

Weaving

Before you weave, make a row of chaining across the bottom of the warp (page 2862). Weaving on this loom is similar to weaving on a simple frame (page 2862). The difference lies in the way you form sheds. To form the first shed, turn the shed stick so it makes a right angle with the warp. This lifts the top layer of warp so you can pass the weft through (photograph 11). Return the shed stick to a flat position and move it to the top of the loom. To form the counter shed with the heddle rod resting in the lower grooves, pull a handful of string heddles toward you. That lifts the warp threads connected to those heddles so you can pass the weft through (photograph 12). Lifting the heddles this way is suitable for tapestry weaving when you are weaving small sections as is usually the case. On occasion, however, the design may call for carrying the weft all the way across the warp, from one selvage to the other. In that case, raise the heddle rod and rest it in the top grooves. This lifts the entire lower layer of warp, and you can pass the weft through the width of the weaving.

Following the directions on page 2863, continue weaving, beating the weft down after each row. When the weaving is completed, make a row of chaining. Cut the weaving off the loom, tying the warp ends together in pairs with an overhand knot.

Geometric pillow

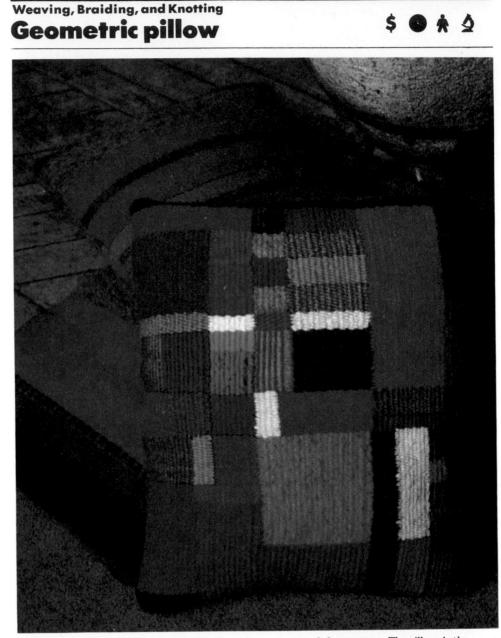

Making a geometric pillow is a practical and ingenious way to use leftover yarns. The pillows in the background have simple horizontal or vertical stripes as part of their designs.

To weave the 16-by-18-inch pillow top shown above, you can use either a simple frame loom (page 2861) or a tapestry frame loom (page 2864). For the warp, you will need about 100 yards of strong cotton or linen yarn, assuming you are using a 26-inch-long loom. For the weft, use wool or acrylic knitting-weight yarn in the colors and amounts indicated in the color key that accompanies Figure I, or small amounts of yarn in whatever colors you prefer. In addition to these materials you will need: a plain piece of paper the same size as the loom (for the cartoon); pencil; ruler; scissors; two 17-by-19-inch pieces of fabric (for the pillow cover); needle and sewing thread to match the fabric; and polyester fiber fill for stuffing.

Weaving

To begin, make the cartoon, or pattern, for the weaving (Figure I). Following the directions on pages 2861 and 2862, warp the loom, making the warp 16 inches wide, with eight warp threads per inch. If you are using the tapestry frame loom,

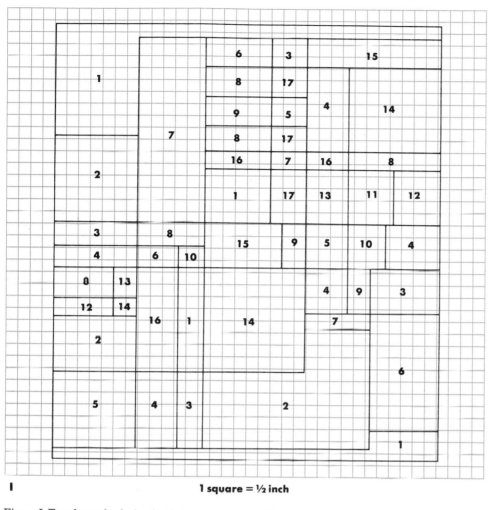

I

1 square = ½ inch

Color key

No.	Color	Yards
1	Blue-black	13
2	Dark reddish-pink	24
3	Dark green	4
4	Orange	8
5	Dark blue	2
6	Purple	8
7	Light pink	24
8	Olive green	7
9	Light blue	3
10	Tan	4
11	Dark blue-green	3
12	Gray-green	3
13	Bright green	3
14	Orange-yellow	7
15	Red	6
16	White	5
17	Light purple	4

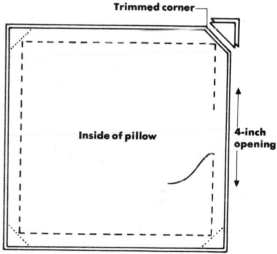

J

Figure J: With right sides facing, sew the pillow fabric together, making a ½-inch seam. Sew along three sides and all four corners, leaving a 4-inch opening along one side. Trim the corners to within ¼ inch of the stitching to reduce bulk.

Figure I: To enlarge the design for the tapestry-woven pillow, use a pencil and ruler to draw a ½-inch grid on paper. Then copy the design, square by square, onto the larger grid, centering it on the paper. Copy the numbers on the enlarged pattern; they indicate the colors in which each area is to be worked.

form the string heddles, following the instructions on page 2865. Make a row of chaining at the bottom edge of the warp (page 2862). Then wind several butterflies as a preparation for the weaving. Tape or pin the cartoon to the back of the loom, and use it as a guide when you weave.

To weave the pillow, create the first shed. Bring the blue-black yarn through the shed, change the shed, and bring the yarn back again. Work in this fashion until you have created the solid-colored portion of the pillow. To weave the portion where the color changes begin, follow the pattern, lifting the appropriate number of warp threads, and bring the weft through. At the end of each color section, cut the weaving yarn, leaving a 1-inch tail dangling. The type of joining used is known as vertical dovetailing, as detailed in the Craftnotes on page 2868. As you work, avoid pulling the weft too tight, and beat it firmly into place after each row so it completely covers the warp. When you have completed the weaving, make a row of chaining at the top of the frame as you did at the bottom. Cut the weaving from the loom and knot the warp ends (page 2863).

Finishing the Pillow

To make the pillow, place the two pieces of backing fabric together, right sides facing and hand- or machine-stitch them together (Figure J). Turn the pillow cover right side out, stuff it with fiber fill and sew the opening closed with tiny stitches. With the right side up, pin the woven pillow top to the fabric pillow, its edges even with the pillow seams, and warp ends tucked in. With tiny stitches, sew the edges of the pillow top to the pillow, catching just a few weft threads with each stitch.

Since tapestries are usually representational or abstract designs, they are woven in sections with different weft yarns, according to how the design motifs and colors fall. There are various techniques for smoothly joining these sections.

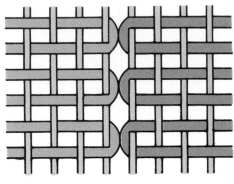

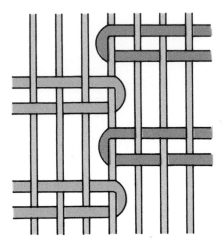

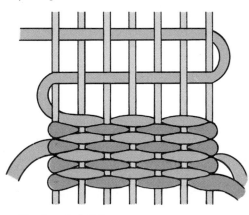

Horizontal stripes:
Weave straight across the warp in plain weave, changing weft colors as needed (above). When you beat the rows down, do so firmly enough to cover the warp completely. Solid horizontal stripes of the color of the weft yarn will be formed.

Vertical slit:
Vertical slits are used to create a straight clean line in weaving. To use this technique, create a shed and bring one weft color from left to right and the other from right to left. Turn each weft around adjacent warp ends and bring each back to its starting point, leaving an unwoven space between the warps. Change the shed and repeat the process, bringing the weft around the same adjacent warps, until the shapes are as large as you want them (above). Do not pull the weft so tightly that the warps are pulled in, unless you want the effect of an open weave. You can use short or long vertical slits as part of the design to give it dimension, or sew them together on the back after you remove the weaving from the loom. You can also use vertical slits to form a woven fringe. Plan the slits carefully so they do not weaken the structure of the fabric.

Vertical dovetail:
This method resembles brick laying and is sometimes called brick interlocking. It forms a decorative rickrack or sawtoothed effect, which can become a part of your design. In one shed, bring one weft from left to right. Change the shed and return the weft to its selvage. Change the shed again and bring the second weft from right to left; change the shed and return the weft to its selvage, making sure it is wrapped around the same warp as the first weft (above).

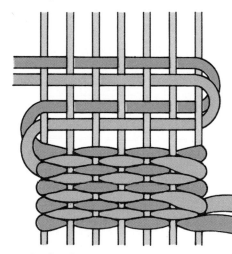

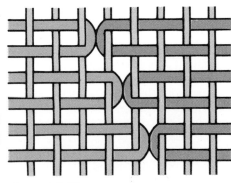

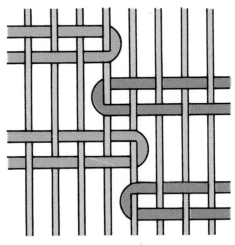

Vertical stripes:
Weave rows of plain weave, alternating two wefts of different colors; beat them down well. Selvages can be treated in a number of ways. Above, in the left selvage one weft (blue) is crossed over the other (brown) so they lock; otherwise the first warp would be continually missed by the blue weft. Another way to handle the selvage is shown on the right.

Diagonal slit:
This technique can be used to create a clearly defined slanting line in a weaving. Create a shed, and bring one weft color from left to right and the other from right to left, following the directions for making the vertical slit. Change the shed, turn the wefts around adjacent warps, and return them to the selvages. As you weave each row, advance one weft and recede the other to form a diagonal line (above).

Diagonal dovetail:
This method is the same as that used for vertical dovetailing, but with the warps of each successive row advancing and receding as for the diagonal slit (above).

WEAVING TECHNIQUES

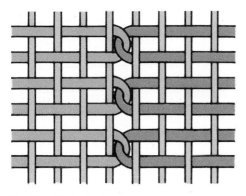

Vertical interlock:

This technique is used to create a minimum amount of thickness at the joining line, which may be straight or slightly jagged, depending on the thickness of the weft yarn and how tightly it is beaten. To create a vertical interlock, form a shed and carry the two weft colors through the same shed from opposite directions, following the directions for making the vertical slit. Where they meet, loop them around each other, however, rather than around the adjacent warp threads (above). To keep the joining line smooth, always loop the wefts around each other in the same direction.

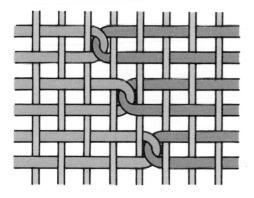

Diagonal interlock:

Work each row the same as the diagonal slit, but interlock the wefts between the adjacent warps (above).

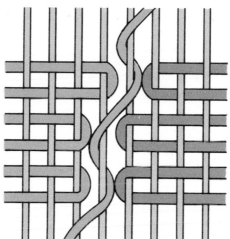

Outlining:

If you would like to accentuate a woven shape, you can outline it with a third weft color. It takes much skill and planning to do this well, however. Weave the shape as you normally would, leaving an empty warp between the two different colored wefts, but receding or advancing the colors as needed. As you weave, form the outline with the third color, spiraling it up around the empty warp to follow the shape being woven. To do this, first weave from left to right over two warps. Then weave from right to left under one warp. Then again weave from right to left over two warps, and so on (above). To outline a partially vertical shape, wind the outline weft up the same warp as many times as needed for the straight line; then advance or recede it over two or more warps to follow the change in shape.

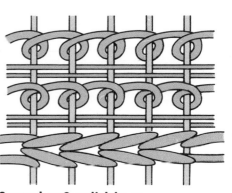

Soumak or Swedish knot:

To impart additional texture to your tapestry, you can use the **soumak** technique, which calls for wrapping the weft around each warp thread, rather than merely passing the weft over or under the warp (above). This necessitates working on a flat warp; so do not form any shed. Working from left to right (top row) or right to left (middle row), loop the weft around the first warp. Bring it forward over two warps, back under one warp, and so on. For structural strength, two rows of plain weave in a thinner yarn are often woven between rows of **soumak**, as shown. You can work the **soumak** in either direction, or alternate from row to row, a common practice that results in a surface that resembles knitting (bottom rows).

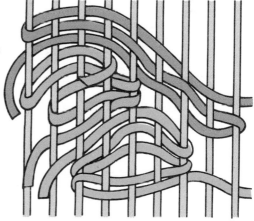

Manipulating wefts:

You can manipulate weft yarn into various shapes, curves, and undulating lines by beating it with a fork or with your fingers. You can push the yarn down firmly, crowding it in to make a pointed end of a shape, then pack it more loosely where the shape swells (above). This gives you great freedom of design.

Tapestries are often pictorial in design, as is this one portraying a flower girl relaxing near an apple-laden tree.

Weaving, Braiding, and Knotting
Apple-tree tapestry

Because there are many vertical shapes in the design, the 12-by-22-inch tapestry shown above was woven sideways. The warp is an unconventional red, chosen because it remains visible in the finished weaving.

Materials
To make the tapestry, you can use any loom set up for plain weave that is at least 18 inches wide and 30 inches long. With a loom that size, you will need approximately 90 yards of red cotton yarn for the warp. For the weft, you will need cotton, wool, or synthetic yarns that are the same weight or slightly thicker than the warp yarn, in the following colors and amounts: gold, 50 yards; blue, 11 yards; olive green, 23 yards; bright blue, 14 yards; plus small amounts of the other colors listed in the color key (Figure K). In addition, to make the cartoon you will need: a plain piece of paper the size of the frame loom; pencil; ruler; and scissors. If you want to mount the finished tapestry on a fabric backing, as I did, you will also need two 16-by-29-inch pieces of fabric, sewing thread to match the warp and the fabric, straight pins, and a sewing needle.

Weaving
Make the cartoon by enlarging the pattern shown in Figure K. Warp the loom, following the directions on pages 2861 or 2865. Make the warp 12 inches wide, with eight warp ends per inch. Make a row of chaining at the bottom of the loom (page 2862). Then, if you are weaving on the tapestry-frame loom, make the string heddles. Wind each of the gold, blue, olive green, and bright blue weft yarns into several small butterflies. Since the areas woven with the remaining colors are small, you can work with short lengths of yarn that are not wound into butterflies.

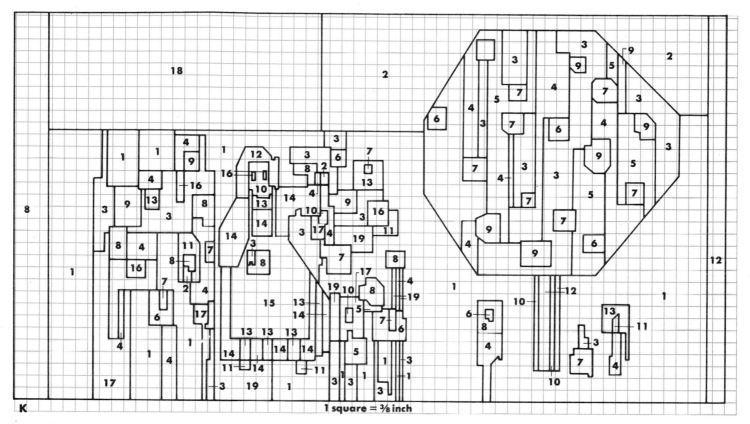

1 square = ⅜ inch

Figure K: To enlarge the design for the apple-tree tapestry, draw a ⅜-inch grid on paper, using a pencil and ruler. Then copy the design, square by square, onto the larger grid, centering it on the paper. Transfer the numbers, which correspond to those in the color key (below), to the enlarged pattern, and follow the outlines of the design as you weave, using the color indicated by the number in each area.

Color key

1	Gold	5	Dark green	10	Light brown	15	Pinkish-white
2	Blue	6	Pink	11	Purple	16	Light blue
3	Olive green	7	Red	12	Dark brown	17	Yellow
4	Green	8	Orange	13	White	18	Bright blue
		9	Salmon pink	14	Shiny white	19	Yellow-green

Tape or pin the cartoon to the loom, behind the warp, so you can use it as a guide to shape each woven area. Weave the design in plain weave, following the weaving directions for the type of loom you are using (pages 2862 through 2865). Referring to the Craftnotes on pages 2868 and 2869, use vertical and diagonal slits, vertical and diagonal dovetails, or vertical and diagonal interlocks to join adjacent areas, depending upon the effect you want. As you weave, beat each row of weft gently so the warp will show through. There should be eight rows of weft per inch, the same as the number of warp threads.

When you have completed the tapestry, make a row of chaining across the top, close to the last row of weaving. Then cut the weaving off the loom, and tie the warp ends together in groups of three using an overhand knot. Trim the fringes thus formed to an even length of about 1½ inches.

Finishing

To mount the tapestry, place the two pieces of backing fabric together, right sides facing. Sew them together all around three sides and four corners, leaving a 4-inch opening for turning. Turn the fabric right side out, fold the edges of the opening ½ inch to the inside, and sew the folded edges together by hand with tiny stitches. Press the backing so it lies flat. Center the tapestry, right side up, on the fabric backing; pin it in place temporarily. Hand sew it to the backing along all four sides. On the two short sides, make a second row of stitches, about 1 inch from the first, catching a group of fringe ends with each stitch (Figure L).

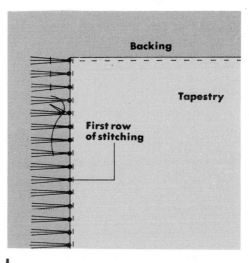

L

Figure L: To mount the finished tapestry on the fabric backing, make a row of tiny stitches along the four sides of the tapestry. Then tack down the fringes by taking a small stitch across each group of warp ends.

Field-of-flowers tapestry

This color-rich wall hanging, reminiscent of a field of flowers, is an advanced project, but one that an experienced weaver can simplify.

The wall hanging shown opposite is unusual in two ways. It was worked upside down so the partially woven fringe could be formed. Otherwise, there would not be enough of a woven foundation to beat successive rows against. In addition, the finished weaving was not cut from the frame. Rather, the frame was disassembled so the warp ends would form loops. The loops at the top edge can be slipped onto a wood dowel for wall mounting or knotted just as the fringe is.

Materials

I recommend using a simple 15-by-24-inch frame loom for this project. Most of the areas you will be weaving are rather small, and it is quite convenient in this case to pick up individual warp threads, rather than relying on heddles. It is much easier to do this type of weaving if the weft yarn is threaded through a tapestry needle, so you should have several of these large, blunt needles on hand. For the warp, I used about 60 yards of white cotton yarn. For the weft, I used a mixture of wool and synthetic yarns in bright colors: pinks, reds, oranges, purples, greens, blues, and white. You will need small amounts of whatever colors you like for the flowers and about 34 yards of a single color for the background areas. To make the full-sized cartoon of the design, you will need a piece of plain paper the size of the loom, ruler, and pencil.

Weaving

Enlarge the pattern for the design (Figure M). Then warp the loom, following the directions on page 2861. The warp should be 10½ inches wide, and have eight threads per inch. Make a row of chaining across the bottom of the warp (page 2862). Then tape or pin the cartoon to the frame upside down. Using the outlines of the cartoon as a guide, weave the shapes in plain weave. Refer to the Craftnotes on pages 2868 and 2869 for the several ways to join adjacent areas. After each row of weaving, beat the weft firmly into place, covering the warp completely. In most cases, you will be using a combination of vertical and diagonal joins to achieve the rounded shapes of the flowers. You can also form the curving lines and lozenge shapes by beating the weft more closely together in some spots.

The end of the solid portion of the design curves inward, as shown in Figure M. To form the curve, omit a few center warp threads in every row. To do this, weave the two side edges separately using two small butterflies. As you work up each side, keep leaving additional center warp threads unwoven, following the lines on the cartoon. When you have completed the curve, begin the woven fringe, working on one section at a time, and again following the cartoon. Leave adjacent fringe sections unjoined, in effect using the vertical slit technique described in the Craftnotes on page 2868.

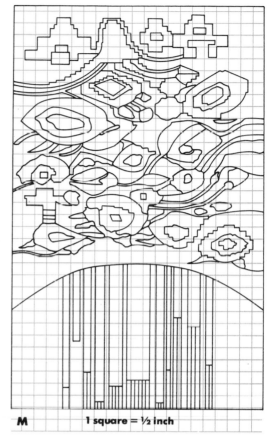

Figure M: To enlarge the design for the field-of-flowers tapestry, draw a ½-inch grid on plain paper, using a pencil and ruler. Then copy the design, square by square, onto the larger grid that you have made, centering it on the paper. You can simplify the design by enlarging only the basic flower shapes, and omitting the details.

M   1 square = ½ inch

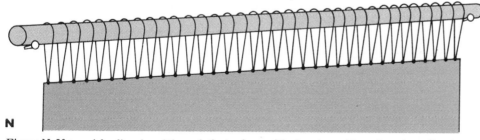

N

Figure N: If you wish, slip a dowel through the top loops of the hanging and hang it on the wall, using two nails, as shown, or two L-shaped brackets.

Finishing

When you have finished the weaving, remove it from the loom either by disassembling the frame and sliding the warps off the strips, as I did, or by leaving the frame intact and cutting the warp ends. To keep the weft from unraveling, tie the warp ends together in pairs, using an overhand knot. Hang the finished weaving as shown in Figure N.

For related projects, see "Inkle Weaving," "Rya and Flossa," "Tablet and Frame Weaving," and "Weaving."

WOVEN TAPESTRIES

A tapestry can be purely ornamental, as in a flat wall hanging. But you can also use tapestry-weaving techniques to produce more unusual or useful items. For example, you could make puppets like the ones pictured at right, which were woven to shape and backed with fabric. Necklaces, bibs, and tiny woven purses with crocheted shoulder straps (below) are other possibilities. The fire-breathing dragon tapestry (bottom), with crocheted tabs and a fabric backing, makes a striking valence when hung across a window. The soft-sculpture column (opposite, far right) was woven flat on a large floor loom, primarily in Swedish knots. Sewn together up the sides, it was attached to a metal ring to get the rounded shape. Tapestry-woven yokes can be incorporated into shirts, like the ones Anita, her husband, Sam, and their son, Sasha, are wearing (opposite).

WRAPPED AND COILED WORK
Basketry Techniques

Basket making is one of the oldest and most universal of all crafts. And the oldest basketry technique is coiling—the construction method of coiling one continuous strand around and on top of itself to form a container. As the foundation core is coiled, it is sewn together with a stitching material called the binder. Early basket makers discovered that if you wrapped the light binding strands around the heavier foundation coils between the stitches, you could increase the strength of the foundation and improve the appearance of the basket. These techniques have attracted modern craftsmen who are experimenting with a variety of new forms, including the use of coiling in sculpture and the use of wrapping on uncoiled work.

Both techniques require the same tools: a cutting instrument and sometimes a needle. Scissors are used unless the foundation material is very thick, as is a rope, when a sharp knife is handier. You will also need a blunt needle for stitching, such as a tapestry or yarn needle, except when you are stitching through the foundation itself. Then a sharp needle may be necessary.

Wrapping
Wrapping one element with another increases rigidity and thus strengthens the construction. Wrapping also improves the surface texture. It allows you to change the direction of the elements, introduce new materials, and, if you choose, add a variety of colors. Hence wrapping is often used to finish the loose ends of woven pieces. They can be gathered and wrapped to hang decoratively. Wrapping can also be used to give a distinctive surface texture to a fiber work. And it can be used to join any group of fibers together. Wrapping is most effective when it is used in a number of units rather than in one or two isolated areas.

Coiling
In coiled basketry, the foundation fiber is usually one continuous coil that begins as a spiral at the bottom and coils around and up to form a container. Since it results from coiling a continuous element, a coiled basket cannot be symmetrical. What appears to be a series of concentric circles is actually a spiral with a definite beginning and end. Thus, the end of a basket coil is often visible and seemingly arbitrary. The decorating pattern incorporated in a coiled basket must accommodate this spiral, which never permits circular bands to begin and end at the same point. The end of a pattern band will always be slightly higher than its beginning.

The material in the foundation can be either a single, continuous element or an amalgam of shorter, finer elements. The foundation must be firm enough to hold a basket shape, yet flexible enough to bend without breaking. And the foundation material must be less pliable than the binder. Traditionally, many plant fibers have been used for the foundation, including grasses, vines, reeds, even pine needles and corn husks. If you harvest these materials, collect them when they have dried, or, if they are green, let them dry thoroughly. If materials you purchase, such as reed, cane, or sea grass, seem too stiff, soak them in cold water until they are flexible enough to use and keep them damp while you are working with them. Wood splints and cane, because they are so inflexible, are suitable only for baskets with slight curves and angles.

Many kinds of cord make a firm, round foundation, including jute, sisal, linen, and cotton. Jute, sisal, and other similar ropes are available in hardware stores; finer jute and sisal twines used for tying packages can be found in variety and stationery stores. If the foundation material is to be covered with wrapping, you can use sturdy cotton cords, including Venetian blind cord and the welting cords used by upholsterers. Some coarse yarns, goat's hair, and horsehair, if tightly twisted, make a functional and beautiful foundation. Basket makers are also experimenting

Sherry De Leon is a weaver who has experimented with many basketry techniques but is especially fond of coiling. She has had a variety of experiences with crafts as a designer for McCall's Needlework & Crafts. *Sherry is the author of a book of basketry techniques.*

Glossary
Binder: The material used to stitch together coils of the foundation material to hold the shape of the basket. It should be strong but flexible, lighter and more pliable than the foundation material.

Coiling: A construction technique of building a form such as a basket by winding one continuous element around into a spiral of rings joined to each other.

Foundation: The material that is coiled around itself to form the basic structure of a coiled basket or to form the central core of other wrapped work. It may be a single continuous element or shorter elements that are joined at intervals to form one continuous coil.

Wrapping: A technique of winding the binder material around the heavier foundation material between stitches, both to increase the strength and to make the surface more decorative. In uncoiled constructions, wrapping wound around a foundation strengthens it, changes the surface texture, and gives form.

In and around the coiled basket are a selection of materials that can be used for wrapping and coiling, including jute, sisal, rope, twine, weaving yarn, reed, and raffia.

with less traditional foundation materials, including plastic tubing, polyester twine, dry-cleaner bags, fabric ropes and strips, ribbons, and twisted paper.

The binder used for stitching the foundation coil together must be more pliable than the foundation but strong enough to withstand the abrasion of stitching and to retain the tension of stitches through the foundation. Test a binder by rubbing your fingernail along a short span, then tug firmly at both ends. If it abrades or breaks, select another. Some plant fibers are strong. Raffia, available in most craft shops, is an excellent binder. Good yarn may be used: rug wool, Persian, tapestry, linen, cotton, and some synthetics. Pearl cotton and silk work well. But avoid highly

CRAFTNOTES:

Starting to coil

A coiled basket is begun in the center of the bottom with the heavier foundation fiber shaped in any configuration: round, oval, rectangular, or some decorative shape. Often, starting such a basket is awkward and may require several attempts before one is successful. Unless the foundation fiber is extremely flexible, cut the end to an

angle. Beginning at this tapered end and continuing to the point where the next coil will begin, wrap the light binder material

several times around the foundation fiber, spacing these wraps to accommodate the coiling stitch that has been selected and securing the end of the binder under its own wraps. For coiling stitches used without wrapping between stitches, space the wraps of the first coil close enough together to allow you to interlace the stitches of the second coil with the initial wraps. After wrapping the tapered end, turn the foundation fiber back on itself to form a closed circle.

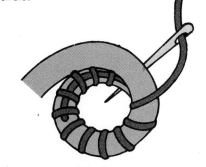

The open end of the foundation fiber should be on the left side so coiling can proceed counterclockwise. As you hold this tight

circle, work the coiling wraps over both the first and the second foundation coils to secure the second foundation coil to the first foundation coil.

Stitching

The stitching of a coiled basket with a lighter binding material maintains the structure, of course, but it also contributes to the design. So the stitch used should be selected with consideration of both. When stitching is spaced widely, the structure is relatively weak. Both the texture and the color of the foundation fiber show, and the stitching itself forms a design over the coiling pattern of the foundation. Alternatively, when the foundation material is completely covered, either by closely spaced stitching or by wrapping between stitches, the structure is stronger, and the texture and pattern more subtle.

Although the rigidity of the basket depends on foundation and binder materials, tight stitching with the binder increases the rigidity. If the foundation is made of many short fibers, stitches must be close to one another to hold the fibers firmly. If the foundation is a continuous element, such as a coiled rope, the stitches need only be close enough to each other to secure the coils. But always the stitches must be frequent enough to maintain the shape of the basket. As the size of a spiral increases, the number of stitches needed increases for each coiled row; the reverse is true when the size decreases. The placement of the stitches should be regular enough to maintain a repetitive surface pattern.

As you stitch coils together, have the outside of the basket facing you so the needle comes from the inside out toward you. This way you do not have to keep turning the basket over to control the placement of each stitch. However, check the inside periodically to be sure the stitches are in place. If you use a different color of thread to temporarily mark the beginning of a spiral, your location in the coil can be determined at a glance.

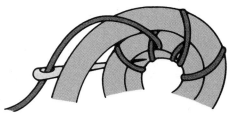

Stitches

Ecuadorian stitch: In this stitch, the binder is wrapped over two rows of the foundation and is intertwined with the stitch lying over the two previous rows (above). This stitch should be used when the foundation is exposed; it is one of the fastest coiling stitches to work. To begin, wrap the first coil as described earlier, spacing the wraps at fairly close intervals. For the second coil, wrap over both coils, again with fairly close spacing matching the wraps of the first coil. Begin the decorative stitching with the third coil. Pass the binder over the outside of both the second and the third coil taking the binder to the inside. Bring the binder out to the front between the second and the first coil passing the binder through the wrap of the previous row. To pass the binder through the wrap of the previous row, on the inside the needle is inserted to the left of the stitch of the previous row, and as it comes to the outside, the needle is to the right of the stitch. Stitches in subsequent coils are placed to give the appearance of spirals on the outside of the basket.

elastic yarns such as knitting worsted.

Material selected for wrapping an uncoiled construction should follow the basic principle of being more pliable than the foundation, but it need not be as firm as the binder used in a basket. This wrapping is commonly worked over many fibers to give them form and rigidity.

The projects that follow include a wrapped plant hanger made with weaving yarn, a wrapped necklace made with six-strand embroidery floss, a coiled basket made with sisal rope and bound with jute, and a wrapped and coiled bread tray made with reed covered with raffia.

COILING

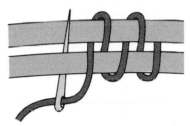

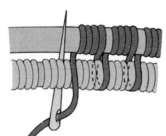

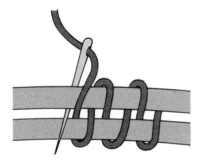

Figure-eight stitch: One of the most common stitches in basketry is the figure eight or Navajo stitch. The binder forms a figure eight around two rows of the foundation. To make the first half of the figure-eight stitch, bring the binder under the first row of the foundation and back out to the front forming a loop around the one foundation row. To

make the second half of the stitch, bring the binder over the top of the second foundation row and out to the front between the first and second foundation rows. The binder forms a figure eight around two foundation rows. On the third (and all subsequent rows) the binder is worked around the new foundation row that you are adding and the foundation row just completed.

To begin this stitch, the first coil of the foundation should be wrapped the space of one stitch apart so that the stitches from the next row will alternate between these wraps over the first coil.

Figure-eight stitch with wrapping: The figure-eight stitch combines readily with foundation wrapping between stitches. To do this, make several wraps over the foundation fiber; then make a stitch. To begin a basket with this method, completely wrap the first coil. Continue to wrap the foundation between stitches. In either version of the figure-eight stitch, individual stitches appear to span only one coil; the actual figure-eight path of the stitch is visible only when the coils are pulled apart slightly.

Adding on

Throughout the stitching of coils, new strands of binding material will have to be added periodically. The technique is the same whether you are changing to a new color or adding more of the same color. But if you are adding a new color, plan where you want the change to occur rather than waiting for the binder to run out. If the stitches, or the stitches and wrapping combined, hide the foundation material, just wrap in the end of the new binder ½ to 1 inch before you make the last stitches with the old binder. When you start to use the new binder, work it over the end of the old binder for ½ to 1 inch; then cut it off.

If the coiling stitches are leaving the foundation material exposed, you can change the binder whenever the binder is on the inside. Wrap several turns of the old binder around a stitch of the previous row. Then take it through the middle of the foundation material, if possible, and cut it off close to the foundation. Start the new length of binder by taking it through the middle of a foundation coil and wrapping it several times around the stitch on the inside that you used previously; then continue to stitch.

How you add onto a single, continuous foundation coil depends on the material used. If possible, work from a long length so the only cut you need to make will be at the end. If this is not possible, you can splice ends by cutting them at angles and gluing or sewing them together. For cords and ropes with several plies, cut the plies at different places, and glue or sew each pair together. Cover any splicing with coiling stitches so you give extra strength to the splice and conceal the joining.

Shaping

The contour of a basket is created by the relationship of each coil to the one that goes before it. Basic shaping involves only pulling in or letting out the foundation material as it is being coiled. Initially, the basket is coiled flat until the base is the desired size. If the basket is to flare out from this base, the first coil of the sides will be placed at an angle to the outer coil of the base. If the basket is to curve in, the first coil will be placed at an angle in from the outer coil of the base. As a guide for such shaping, place the base against a curved shape to find the position for the next coil. Continue setting subsequent coil rows at an angle until the basket is shaped. If the sides then go straight up, place coils on top of one another. At the top of the basket, you can pull in or flare out, depending on how you angle the coiled rows.

Finishing

To offset the lack of symmetry of the top of a spiral, plan to end the coil at the end of a round. Cut the foundation material off at that point. Taper this end as you did the beginning, and glue it if necessary. Continue stitching to the end; then anchor the binder by wrapping over it. Cut off the end of the binder close to the stitching.

Weaving, Braiding, and Knotting
Wrapped necklace

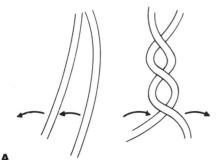

Embroidery floss in various pastel colors forms both the foundation material and the wrapped binder for this unusual necklace.

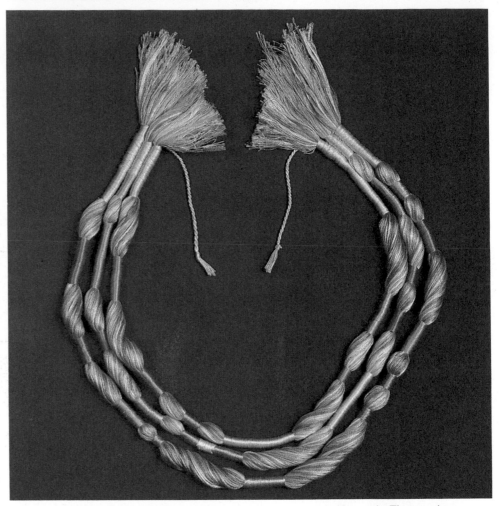

The closure of the necklace is formed by adding a twisted cord on each side as a tie. These are incorporated in two of the end wraps; the three end wraps on each side are stitched together.

A
Figure A: To make a twisted cord, anchor four 12-inch lengths of embroidery floss to a doorknob or under a C-clamp. Hold two of the lengths in each hand. Twist each pair counterclockwise (left) while twisting the pairs together clockwise (right). When the entire length is twisted tight and even, tie each end with an overhand knot. Then knot the twisted cord twice in the center, and cut between the center knots to get the two cords needed.

The necklace shown above has three loops, each made of wrapped embroidery floss. A variety of colors were used. To make this necklace, you will need the following number of 7-yard skeins of six-strand embroidery floss: 3 apricot, 3 celadon green, 4 pale olive green, 3 ice blue, 4 sky blue, 4 light yellow, 5 coral, and 5 lavender. You will also need a tape measure, scissors, a sharp needle, and a means of anchoring the foundation threads while you are wrapping them. These threads can be anchored in a closed drawer, under a C-clamp, or tied to a doorknob.

Each of the three necklace loops are made in the same way, but each is a different length. For these loops, the floss should be cut to 24, 26, and 28 inches respectively. While it is possible to separate the floss into six strands, here each length refers to the six strands together as one unit. For each necklace loop, cut 40 to 45 lengths, including some of each color, proportionate to the skeins on hand. This is easiest if each color is cut to length separately and then the loops are assembled. Carefully gather the lengths for each loop, being careful not to twist or tangle the floss.

From floss that remains, select the color to be used for the long end wraps at the back of the necklace—the largest amount of any single color on display. From this color, cut four lengths of floss, each 12 inches long, for the twisted tie cords. Tie these lengths together with an overhand knot at one end; anchor that end. Holding two lengths in each hand, twist each pair counterclockwise while you twist them together clockwise (Figure A, opposite). Continue twisting until the whole length is tight and even; then tie an overhand knot in that end. In the center of the twisted cord, tie two more overhand knots close together. Cut the cord between these center knots.

Wrapping is easier to do if the foundation material is under tension. Begin with the shortest loop. Gather the floss lengths together, and tie an overhand knot at one end. Anchor the overhand knot of the foundation floss in a closed drawer, on a doorknob, or under a C-clamp, with the loop to be wrapped toward you (photograph 1). To add maximum strength, wrapping should be done tightly with each wrap close to the next. Ends of the wrapping binder are secured underneath themselves. As you wrap, twist the foundation floss to keep it compact and to add interest to areas left unwrapped. Be sure to twist in the same direction throughout.

For the short lengths of wrapping, the easiest method of securing the end requires no tools. Cut the binder cord a bit longer than you need for wrapping. If this length seems unwieldy, make a butterfly of it so it will be easier to handle (photograph 2). Holding the foundation loop under tension in one hand, lay the end of the binder cord on top of the foundation, parallel with it and extending slightly beyond where the wrapping is to stop; double the binder cord back, leaving a loop beyond the stopping point (Figure B, left). Start wrapping opposite this loop. Keep your thumb on the doubled binder cords while you wrap the binder around the foundation and the doubled binder cord at the same time (Figure B, center). Wrap tightly and with even tension, leaving no foundation visible. At the stopping point, insert the end of the wrapped binder through the loop. Hold this end as you gently

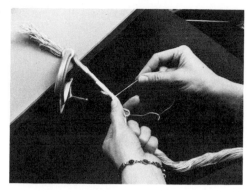

1: To wrap a foundation of embroidery floss under tension, anchor one end under a C-clamp. You can also clamp it in a door or tie it to a doorknob. As you wrap the foundation, twist it as shown while you hold it taut.

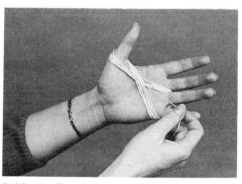

2: A butterfly will let you hold a long length of floss without tangling it. Wrap the thread around your hand in a figure-eight shape.

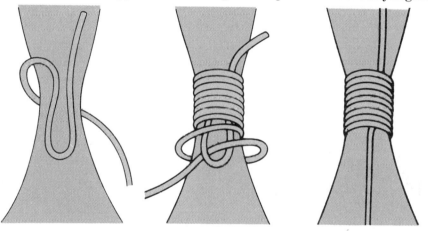

B

Figure B: To begin and end a short span of wrapping, start with the end of the binder beyond the beginning of the wrapping. A bit below where you plan to stop the wrapping, double the binder back parallel with the foundation floss (left). Start wrapping at the far side, working around both the foundation and the binder end. When you reach the stopping point, insert the second end of the binder through the loop you have made (center). Pull on the beginning end of the binder. This pulls the loop and the second end of the binder up under the wrapping (right). Trim the ends of binder close to the wrapping.

pull on the beginning end of binder. This will gradually pull the loop and the opposite binder end under the wrapping (Figure B, right). Pull until you are sure the end is anchored; then cut off both ends close to the wrapping.

Using various colors and lengths of floss as the binder, wrap other sections of the foundation floss. Leave some areas unwrapped for ½ to 2 inches, and wrap some areas for ½ to 2 inches. When you are 3 or 4 inches from an end of the foundation floss, use the finishing color of floss to start wrapping that end. As you wrap toward the end, lay in the center knot of one twisted cord parallel with the floss foundation (Figure C). Anchor the twisted cord by continuing to wrap over the cord and the foundation and finish wrapping to within 2 inches of the foundation ends. Remove the other end of the foundation floss from its anchor, and undo the overhand knot at that point. Anchor the completed end. Then wrap the second end in the same way as the first, including the other twisted cord.

Wrap the other two cords of the necklace and their ends, but do not include a twisted cord in the end wrappings. Vary the length and color of wrapped areas

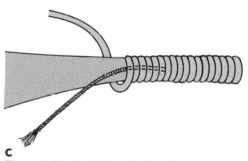

C

Figure C: To attach the twisted cord that will serve as the closure tie, lay it parallel to the foundation and wrap over its end knot. Continue wrapping over both the cord and the foundation.

from one cord to another for a variety in each of the three cords.

To join the three sections, thread the finishing color of floss in a needle, and work a variation of the figure-eight stitch around the three wrapped ends on each side of the necklace (Figure D). Work these stitches from the inner edge to the outer edge of the three wrappings. Finally, trim the loose ends of the foundation floss at an angle as shown in photograph 3.

3: Trim the free ends of the bundles of foundation floss at an angle—they form a fringe at the back of the necklace.

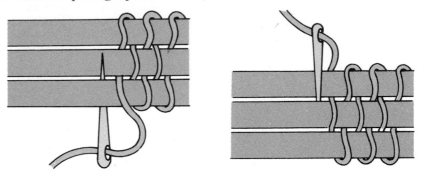

D

Figure D: To join the three loops of the necklace to each other, work a variation of the figure-eight stitch around the wrapping at the ends of the three parts. Use matching floss for the stitches.

E

Figure E: To begin a long section of wrapping, fold the beginning end of the binder in and parallel to the foundation material. Secure it under the beginning wraps.

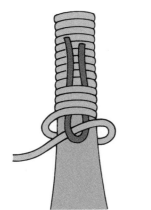

F

Figure F: To end a long section of wrapping, fold a short piece of lighter-weight thread in half, and lay it parallel to the foundation. Let the ends project above the previous wrapping and the loop extend beyond where the wrapping will end. At the end of the wrapping, put the end of the binder through the loop. Pull gently on the ends of the loop until the binder end is pulled out through the wrapping. Trim this end close to the wrapping.

Weaving, Braiding, and Knotting
Plant hanger

A wrapped and tied plant hanger, as shown opposite, provides an attractive way to display any trailing plant. If you like, use yarn in colors that will match the decor of the room where the plant will be hung. To make the plant hanger shown, you will need about 8 ounces of a 3-ply weaving yarn in a natural color for the foundation and 1 to 2 ounces each of light blue, olive green, and brown for the wrapping. You will also need: a tape measure; scissors; yarn needle; and some means of anchoring the foundation yarn.

For this foundation, cut sixty-five 4½-yard lengths of natural-color yarn. Gather these lengths together with the ends fairly even and fold them in half. Mark the midpoints with a piece of contrasting color yarn and unfold them. Temporarily anchor the foundation cords while you wrap at the midpoint. To anchor, you can clamp the yarn to a table with a C-clamp, hold it in a closed drawer, or tie it to a doorknob.

To make the strong hanging loop, use one of the three colors of yarn as the binder (photograph 4). Wrap the binder around the foundation yarn for a continuous 8 inches, 4 inches on either side of the midpoint.

To wrap such a long area, the loop method described previously (page 2881) is not manageable. Instead, begin by folding in the end of the binder cord parallel to the foundation and down from the point where you start to wrap (Figure E). Wrap around the foundation, concealing the end of the binder cord. At the other end of the wrap, there are two methods of securing the second end of the binder. The first is to wrap to the stopping point, thread the end of the binder through a needle, then insert the needle under the wrapping, pulling it out between wraps a short distance up. Pull the binder tight and trim the end. The second method makes use of a short length of a lighter thread and works on the loop principle. Shortly before the wrap is finished, fold a lighter-weight thread in half and lay it in, parallel to the foundation. Let the two thread ends project above the previous wrapping, with the loop extending beyond the stopping point (Figure F). Continue wrapping over both the foundation and the thread to the stopping point. Put the binder end through the loop. Pull gently on the thread ends until the loop pulls the binder end up under the wrapping. Pull the loop until both it and the binder end come through the wrapping. Trim off the binder end.

When the 8 inches have been wrapped, undo the anchoring and refold the foundation at the midpoint. Using all the foundation yarn, tie an overhand knot just below the wrapping (Figure G and photograph 4). Only the wrapped hanging loop should be visible above the knot.

G
Figure G: Using all the lengths of foundation yarn, tie them together with an overhand knot just below the midpoint wrapping to make a strong loop.

This plant hanger is made by wrapping different colored weaving yarns around a foundation of a group of natural-colored yarn.

4: Only the wrapped hanging loop is visible above the overhand knot at the top of the plant hanger.

Anchor the hanging loop and divide the foundation yarn into five groups approximately equal. Varying the three colors of binder yarns, wrap sections of the five foundation divisions at irregular intervals. As you work with each division, twist the foundation yarns to keep them compact and to add interest in the unwrapped sections. Always twist in the same direction. You can add interest to the wrapping by occasionally subdividing a foundation division. Wrap only some of the yarn, letting some hang loose until the next wrapping. Or divide the yarn into two or three subdivisions, and wrap each separately. Then twist them together when they are wrapped. Or divide the yarn into subdivisions and wrap each with a different

5: Each of the five divisions of the foundation yarn can be wrapped completely, wrapped partially, or not wrapped at all, using any or all of the three binder colors.

color. Photograph 5 shows a variety of wrapping methods on the five divisions.

When each of the divisions is 32 inches long, tie an overhand knot in each one. Below the knots, divide each of the five divisions in half. Take half from one and half from the adjacent division, and tie an overhand knot 4 inches below the previous knot (Figure H). Repeat all around until you have five new divisions. In the 4-inch space between knots, use the three binder yarns to wrap each of the ten divisions. Wrap some of these completely, wrap some half in one color and half in another, and leave some unwrapped.

Below the last knots, use one color of binder yarn to wrap each of the five divisions separately for 4 inches. Then gather all the foundation yarns together, and tie an overhand knot at the bottom of the wrappings. This is where the pot and its saucer will be placed. Trim straggling ends below the last knot if necessary, but not to the point where they are all even. Tie an overhand knot at the end of each length of foundation yarn to add fullness to the tassel.

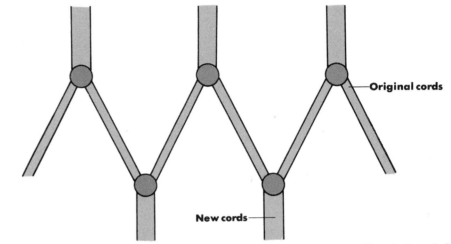

H
Figure H: To make the web in which the plant's pot and saucer will sit, tie an overhand knot in the end of each section when it is 32 inches long. Then divide each in half. Take half from one section and half from the adjacent section and tie an overhand knot 4 inches below the previous knots. Repeat all around until you have five new divisions. Wrap each of the ten 4-inch sections in any of the three binder colors. Below the last knots, wrap 4 inches of each of the five new sections. Gather all of the foundation yarns together, and tie them with an overhand knot at the bottom of the wrapping.

Weaving, Braiding, and Knotting
Sisal basket
$ 🗓 🧍 🦺

The basket shown opposite and on page 2876 was made using sisal rope for the foundation and dark brown jute for the binder. The jute is worked in the Ecuadorian stitch, described in the Craftnotes on pages 2878 and 2879. It creates an interesting pattern against the light natural coloring of the sisal.

To make the basket, you will need: one 100-foot coil of ⅜-inch sisal rope; 6 to 8 ounces of 3/16-inch, 2-ply brown jute; a plastic ring ¾ inch in diameter (available at variety stores); scissors; mat knife; yarn needle; and white glue.

Since forming a tight circle with bulky sisal rope is difficult, an alternative is to coil the foundation rope around a disk or ring. (This leaves a small hole in the bottom.) Using the jute binder, work a buttonhole stitch around the plastic ring to completely cover it (Figure I). To start the coil, taper the end of the sisal rope, and glue it to prevent unraveling. Coil the rope counterclockwise around the buttonhole stitches on the ring, wrapping the binder over the rope and through the buttonhole stitches at close intervals (Figure J). For the second round, coil the rope beside the first round, and wrap the binder over both rounds (photograph 6). For the third round and all subsequent rounds, begin using the Ecuadorian stitch. In this stitch, the needle with binder is brought to the left of the stitch below it (photograph 7 and Craftnotes, pages 2878 and 2879). The needle is then pulled out on the front to the right of the stitch below (photograph 8).

This coiled basket is sisal rope stitched with the Ecuadorian stitch using dark brown jute. Since the rope is so thick, the basket was begun by stitching the jute around a plastic ring to which the sisal rope was then attached.

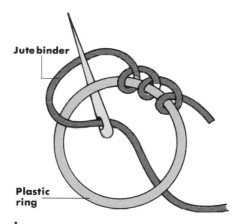

Jute binder

Plastic ring

I
Figure I: Using jute binder, work the buttonhole stitch around the plastic ring that is used to start a basket spiral in the middle of the bottom. Work the stitches close together so they almost completely cover the ring.

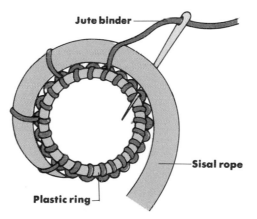

Jute binder

Sisal rope

Plastic ring

J
Figure J: To begin the rope coil, taper the end of the sisal, and glue it to prevent unraveling. Attach the coil of rope to the ring by stitching around it and through the buttonhole stitches made previously.

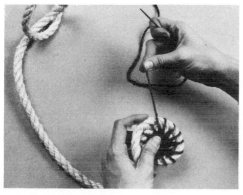

6: To form the second round, coil the rope around the first round; then wrap the jute binder over both rounds and through the buttonhole stitches at the center.

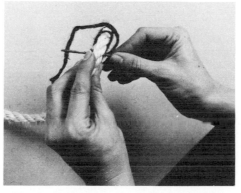

7: For the third round start the Ecuadorian stitch, described in the Craftnotes (page 2878 and 2879). Here, the needle is being taken to the back and to the left of the stitch previously made.

8: Then, the needle is pulled out to the front and to the right of the stitch previously made. The previous stitch helps to hold the stitch being made in place so it does not slip.

2885

Continue coiling the sisal rope and stitching it in place in a flat disk shape for 11 rounds. At the 12th round, begin to shape the basket sides by moving the rope coil up and out slightly. On this round, increase the number of stitches by five or six by taking the extras at intervals between the existing stitches. The sides of the basket will need the extra support of these additional stitches. For rounds 13 through 19, shape the basket sides by placing the rope directly on top of the previous coils so the sides are perpendicular to the bottom of the basket. For rounds 20 through 22, place the rope slightly to the inside of the previous rows so the top of the basket will curve in. At the start of round 23, pull out a curve of sisal rope about 6 inches long to make a handle. To avoid stitching over the handle, skip the next two or three stitches and take the binder across to the stitch at the other end of the handle. Continue stitching until you are halfway around the basket; then form another handle the same way. Place round 24 on top of round 23. At the handles, stitch round 24 into round 22. For the final round, place the rope outside of the previous round so the top of the basket flares out slightly. Just before you reach the end of this round, cut a taper at the end of the rope, as you did at the beginning, and glue it to the previous round. Secure the rope end with the last stitches of the binder.

Weaving, Braiding, and Knotting
Reed-and-raffia bread tray

This brightly colored bread tray is made with a combination of wrapping and coiling in three colors of raffia over a foundation of reed.

The bread tray shown above is made of raffia in three different colors, wrapped and stitched around a coiled reed. To make this tray, you will need one bundle of No. 3 reed, and red, blue, and green raffia. Raffia is sold with assorted colors packed in one-pound bags—depending on how much of any one color you want to use, you will need one or two bags. You will also need a craft knife, scissors, and tapestry needle. To start the tray, cut one end of one reed at an angle. To get a very tiny circle for the start, soak the cut end of the reed in cold water until it is pliable. Thread a length of red raffia in the tapestry needle. Since raffia is a natural material (taken from the raffia palm tree in Madagascar) the width of each piece will vary. You may find it necessary to split a piece of raffia lengthwise to get a thin enough strip to make a tiny circle. Wrap the tapered end of the reed with the raffia so the reed does not show, wrapping just far enough for the end of the reed to be doubled snugly against itself (Figure K). Then hold the circle in place with a figure-eight stitch (page 2879). Use the figure-eight stitch with wrapping throughout the tray. At the beginning, when the circle is very small, wrap only once or twice between stitches. As the circle becomes larger, wrap three or four times between stitches. Wrap and stitch with the red raffia until the circle measures 9½ inches in diameter (photograph 9).

Change to the blue raffia. To start a new color or a new length of raffia of the same color, place the end of the new raffia parallel to the reed a short distance before the end of the old length (Figure L, top). Continue wrapping and stitching with the old length to secure the end of the new. Then thread the needle with the new length and begin to wrap over the end of the old (Figure L, bottom). This conceals the end of the old length. Wrap and stitch with the blue raffia for three rounds.

Then shape the sides of the tray for the next five rounds by placing each coil on top of the previous coil. Change to the green raffia and pull the sides of the tray in

K
Figure K: To begin the tray, taper the end of a reed and soak it in cold water until it is soft enough to be folded on top of itself. Then wrap the end, fold, and stitch the bend together with raffia.

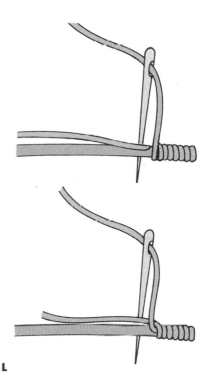

L
Figure L: To start a new color, lay an end of raffia parallel to the reed before you finish wrapping the old color (top). Continue wrapping and stitching with the old color until you have secured the end of the new color. Then thread the needle with the new color, and lay the end of the old parallel to the reed. As you begin to work with the new color, secure and conceal the end of the old color under the wrapping (bottom).

9: To make a bread tray, red raffia is used to wrap and stitch reed into a coil until the circle measures 9½ inches. Then, blue raffia is used for eight rounds and green for five. One final round of red provides a decorative edge.

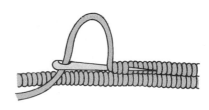

M
Figure M: To secure the outside end of the binder, insert the needle under the last several wrapping stitches, and pull the binder under them. Clip the excess binder close to the wrapping.

for five more rounds. For the final round, use red raffia. Taper the end of the reed again and wrap it to the very end. Secure this end of the binder by running the needle under the last several stitches and pulling the binder out (Figure M). Trim the end of the binder close to the wrapping.

For related crafts, see "Basketry" and "Rope Knotting."

WYCINANKI
Shear Fun from Poland

After graduating from Monmouth College, New Jersey, Diane Braun taught art in elementary schools. She now lives in East Hampton, New York, where she is a member of the South Fork Craftsmen's Guild. Diane and her husband, Jim, are enthusiastic sailors and have restored a 1932 Herreshoff racing boat.

The decorative paper cuttings known as wycinanki (vee-chee-NON-key) appeared among the peasants of east-central Poland less than a century ago. At a time when many folk arts were being stifled by the industrial revolution, this delicate craft flourished. In Polish hamlets and the countryside (the shaded part of the map in Figure A, page 2890, shows the heartland of the craft), a number of regional styles were established. Today wycinanki is attracting worldwide attention for its colorful and imaginative designs.

There are two major branches of the craft: exquisitely filigreed silhouettes of a single color, usually cut in geometrical designs, and brilliant pictorial découpage works—called Łowicz (WA-vitch) for their place of origin—made by layering variously colored papers. The silhouettes, cut from folded paper, sometimes are the shapes of stars, leaves, flowers, trees, peacocks, and roosters. Layered cutouts include these motifs plus stylized human figures, flowers, and bucolic scenes.

The examples of wycinanki pictured opposite and below are advanced works, but all the techniques used are demonstrated in the simpler projects that follow. Dexterity with scissors, skill in folding paper, and the ability to combine shapes and

Three examples of Polish wycinanki (paper cutting) show how exquisite the craft can be. Designs like the bird-and-flower motif opposite can be executed with little experience. The more difficult garden scene (above top) and pastoral scene (above) are done in the tradition of the Łowicz region. All were made by carefully cutting bits of colored paper and assembling them with glue.

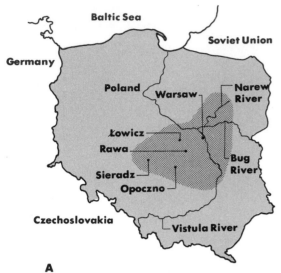

A

Figure A: The shading on this map of Poland indicates the regions where the art of wycinanki is most widely practiced.

colors effectively all come with practice.

In Poland, the tool used for cutting paper is a heavy sheep shears. You could do the work with two pairs of ordinary scissors, one at least 6 inches long and strong enough to cut through several folds of paper, the other a small embroidery scissors for fine cuts. (For special effects, you might want to try manicure scissors or pinking shears, but remember that cutting paper will dull any scissors rapidly.)

For layering and mounting the cutouts, you can use either liquid white glue or rubber cement. I prefer rubber cement because any excess can be removed with a pencil eraser. You can use any kind of paper for the cutouts, including newspaper. Tissue paper is recommended for multiple images and is beautiful cut into lacy snowflakes and similar designs. Gift-wrap and lightweight poster paper are easy to cut, even in multiple thicknesses. You might want to try textured stationery papers, shelving paper, or origami paper. Aluminum foil can be used as a border or insert, but it tears too easily to be used in elaborate work.

The Poles make wycinanki to decorate their homes. Their work is striking when used as a border decoration on a whitewashed wall. You can use your cutouts as mobiles, window decorations, Christmas ornaments, greeting cards, party favors, place mats, or doilies.

Paper Folding and Cutting
A chain of animals

In the elaborate Łowicz designs pictured on page 2888, the most difficult part to make was the bottom border. The remainder of each composition consists of paper cutouts; the art in these pictures is in the combination of shapes and colors rather than in any crafting technique.

To show how a continuously repeating lower border is made, and at the same time suggest a project for children, I asked my son to choose a design and use it to demonstrate folding and cutting. He chose a cat. Other animals, birds, fishes, flowers, funny faces, human figures, and geometrical designs can be cut by following the same simple techniques.

1: To start making the animal chain pictured opposite, fold a long, narrow strip of paper accordion-style at 2-inch intervals. The number of folds you make will determine the number of figures in your chain. The paper strip shown was 3 inches wide.

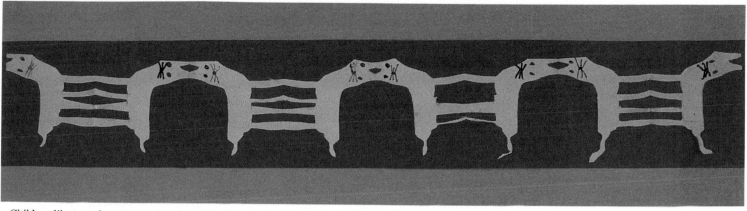

Children like to make paper cutout chains like this one depicting eight cats joined ear to ear and paw to paw. The cats (or other figures) can be made with a few folds and scissor cuts in a strip of paper. Decoration with crayons, inks, or paints is optional.

To make the chain of cats pictured above, cut a strip of poster paper 3 by 16 inches. Fold it accordion-style at 2-inch intervals (photograph 1). Make each leaf the same size and keep the sides even. Press the folds together, making sure they are aligned, and draw the design on the top leaf, with folds at bottom and top edges (photograph 2). Make the figure large enough so a substantial amount—here the ears and feet—touches folded edges so the figures will remain joined when the strip is opened. Sean's cat, with its flat-tipped ears and feet, is shown in Figure B. Holding the paper accordion snugly, cut along the pencil outline (photograph 3). Then, holding only the top leaf, gently lift to open the chain of figures (photograph 4).

Traditional wycinanki is a paper craft that excludes all secondary materials. A paper chain, for example, would be decorated with small paper cutouts. But children also like to decorate paper chains with crayons, paint, or felt-tipped pens. If the chain is mounted, such colors should be added only after the adhesive has dried. The moisture in many glues will make paints or inks run.

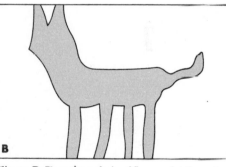

Figure B: To make a chain of figures, let the pattern that was traced on the top layer of a paper accordion overlap both folded edges. The figures will be joined at the overlapped points.

2: On the top leaf, draw a cat like the one shown in Figure B or any other design you like that will overlap the folded edges.

3: Without unfolding the strip, cut out the figure you have drawn. Be sure to leave part of the top and bottom edges uncut to hold the chain intact.

4: Gently lift the top layer of the paper until you have opened the entire chain. If the cut edges cling to each other, separate them with care.

An airy star with interior cutouts, perhaps for a Christmas tree or just for good behavior, takes little skill to make, but it illustrates the basic techniques used in more elaborate geometric shapes.

Paper Folding and Cutting
A five-pointed star

Successful geometric wycinanki depends as much on folding as on cutting. A number of standard folding variations have been developed. Among the most useful and popular shapes are five-pointed stars and hexagons. Both make pleasing Christmas ornaments and snowflake motifs. You can make stars resembling the one pictured at left (no two are ever exactly alike) by folding a piece of paper in the sequence shown in Figures C through F, then cutting the folded paper as shown in Figure G. Begin by cutting a piece of decorative paper into a square. A 3-inch square is about the smallest worth cutting, and this only if you use tissue paper; folding thick paper into a small area distorts the design and makes cutting difficult. You can, of course, make very large geometric wycinanki, even wall-sized compositions. The larger the scale, the thicker the paper you can use. Fold the square in

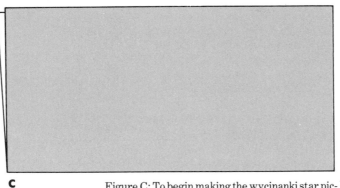

C

Figure C: To begin making the wycinanki star pictured above, fold a square sheet of paper in half, bringing the bottom edge up so it meets the top.

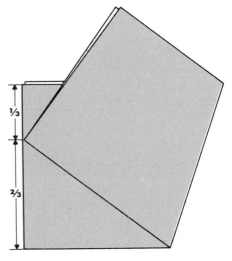

D

Figure D: Fold the paper for the star again, bringing the lower right corner to a point on the left edge two-thirds of the way up from the bottom.

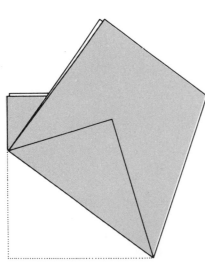

E

Figure E: Continue folding by bringing the triangle at the lower left-hand corner (represented by the dotted line) up to the right, creasing it along the edge produced by the previous fold.

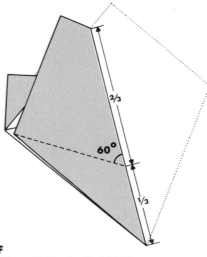

F

Figure F: For the final fold for the star, bring the right side over the left as far as the edge created in the previous step. Then cut across the folded paper from a point one third of the way up the right edge to the lowest point that protrudes from the left edge (dashed line).

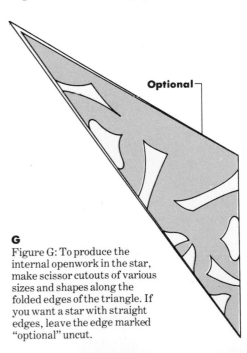

G

Figure G: To produce the internal openwork in the star, make scissor cutouts of various sizes and shapes along the folded edges of the triangle. If you want a star with straight edges, leave the edge marked "optional" uncut.

2892

Additional decorative cutouts based on the star- or pentagon fold suggest the endless array of designs that it is possible to make.

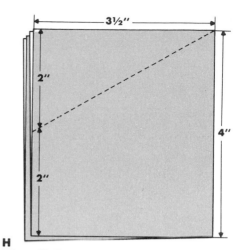

Figure H: To make a hexagon for a snowflake design, start with a sheet of paper 8 by 6 15/16 inches. Fold it in half twice so the corner where the folds converge is at the lower right, and the shorter edges of the rectangle are at the top and bottom. Cut across the folded paper from the upper right corner to the middle of the left edge (dashed line).

half, keeping the folded edge at the bottom (Figure C). Measure up along the left edge two-thirds of the way to the top, and fold the paper again so the lower right corner meets this point (Figure D). To complete the folding, follow the steps shown in Figures E and F. Holding the folded shape tightly, cut across the paper at about a 60-degree angle, as shown in Figure F. This cut should begin about one-third of the way up the right edge and should end at the lowest protruding point on the left edge. (As shown above, varying the angle of this cut will change the shape of the star. If you begin your cut nearer the bottom, you will get a sharp-pointed star; if you begin higher up, the points will be shorter, and if you make your cut perpendicular to the right edge, you will no longer have a star but a pentagon.) Discard the portion of the folded paper above the cut, and keep the triangle that remains, but do not unfold it yet.

With an embroidery scissors, make small cutouts along the folded edges of the triangle. Leave enough of each edge intact to avoid cutting the star in half, and do not connect one cutout section with another. Cuts can be triangular, square, crescent-shaped, or irregular. Figure G illustrates some typical cuts. If you do not want the outside edge of the star to be irregular, do not make any cuts along the unfolded edge (marked optional in Figure G). When you have made a few cuts, unfold the triangle to see how the design is progressing. If you like what you see, stop, but if more decoration is needed, refold the star along the original creases and resume cutting.

Snowflakes

Snowflakes are as easy to make as stars. Cutting is done the same way, but since the snowflakes are based on hexagons rather than pentagons, the folding is different. For an equal-sided hexagon, start with a sheet of paper 8 by 6 15/16 inches (8 by 7 is close enough for a children's project). Fold it in half twice, so the folded edges are at the bottom and right, with the shorter edge at the top. As shown in Figure H, cut from the top folded corner to the middle of the opposite unfolded edge. Fold the remaining shape to form a triangle as shown in Figures I and J. Make the cutouts in the edges of the triangle as before (opposite).

Finished stars and snowflakes can be suspended with thread. If you like, you can iron out the creases and mount the design on other paper.

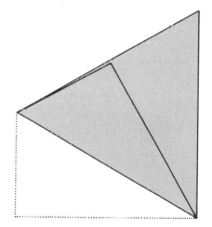

Figure I: Fold the paper, now a trapezoid in shape, along a line running from the lower right corner to the upper left corner, forming a triangle.

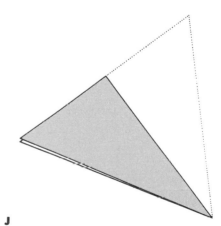

Figure J: Then fold the triangle in half along the center edge produced in the previous step.

Paper Folding and Cutting
A tree of life

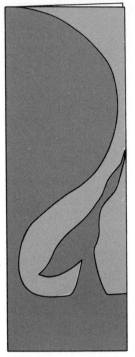

K
Figure K: To make the tree of life pictured at right, fold a rectangular sheet of paper in half lengthwise. Draw the design, keeping in mind that the folded edge at the left will become the center of a symmetrical pattern. Cut away the waste shown in beige.

L
Figure L: To start the openwork in the tree, cut additional curving lines within its outline. Follow the pattern above; areas to be removed are shown in beige. Enlarge each cut to a width of 1/16 to 1/8 inch by removing a thin strip of paper along one side of the cut. Finally, remove the opening beneath the bird to form its thin legs.

A tree silhouette with a pair of birds requires few folds but much decorative snipping.

The tree-of-life motif has far-ranging possibilities, as these modern variations show.

Additional motifs which can be incorporated in a tree-of-life design include these plants, birds, human figures, and abstract designs.

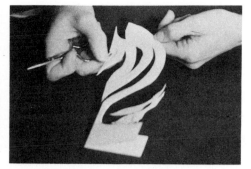

5: To make space for snipping the decorative edges that line the openings in the tree of life, pull the center of the paper gently to the left.

6: Cut tiny decorative designs along all the edges created by the previous cuts.

M

Figure M: To complete the tree, cut tiny designs into the edges produced by earlier scissor cuts. Do not try to follow this drawing precisely; every tree should be different. The dashed lines represent secondary folds that can be made to produce symmetrical openwork in the decorative base.

One of the commonest wycinanki motifs is the traditional tree of life or tree of the world, pictured opposite. A tree is well suited to symmetrical treatment, and the foliage is easily simulated in snipped paper. Trees serve as a sort of good-luck charm. To emphasize their life symbolism, they are often accompanied by storks or lovebirds. The three tree silhouettes pictured are representative and can be made without special skill, though meticulous cutting is required. Once you have made one or two, you will be able to produce original designs.

To begin, fold a rectangular sheet of paper in half lengthwise, and copy the design in Figure K on one side of the paper. (Alternative motifs are shown above.) The sheet I used measured 5 by 7⅛ inches, but unless you want to trace the design, the size is immaterial. The folded edge is at the left in Figure K. Cut the waste from the double thickness of paper (beige in Figure K). Next, cut the internal curving lines (Figure L). The longest cut, which should be made first, begins near the center of the folded edge and moves upward, parallel with and about ½ inch to the left of the edge of the tree. This cut should end about ½ inch in from the folded edge. If this cut extended all the way back to the folded edge, the entire center of the tree would be freed. Mistakes are not irreparable, however; disconnected sections can be taped back in place. The second cut begins about an inch below the top of the folded edge and curves downward ½ inch to the left of the first cut. End it, too, about ½ inch short of the fold. The third cut proceeds upward like the first, the fourth like the second. The fifth is a complete cutout in the shape of half a heart, the small central decoration.

Enlarge all the scissor cuts (except the heart) to a width of 1/16 to 1/8 inch by trimming away a narrow strip of paper along the length of each (Figure L). Also cut out the opening beneath the bird to make its legs. This delicate cut requires care because there is no access from the edge (the tip of the scissors must be pushed through the paper). For cuts like this, I sometimes use a craft knife.

With structural cuts completed, decorative snipping can begin. If you pull the center of the tree gently toward the left, the slits will open a bit and give you more room to work (photograph 5). Use an embroidery scissors to decorate the edges of all the strips (photograph 6 and Figure M). It is not necessary to reproduce Figure M exactly; the shapes of the snips should vary from one tree to the next. After you complete the tree, make similar cutouts in the bird's tail and in the foreground. Dashed lines in Figure M indicate where you might make additional folds for secondary cuts in the base.

Paper Folding and Cutting
A disk mobile

A mobile is a display of geometric wycinanki. The disk that dominates the assemblage, though quite elaborate, was cut in a few seconds through 16 layers of folded paper. Star forms, described on pages 2892 and 2893, complete the mobile.

Many new applications of wycinanki are being discovered. One I like is the wycinanki mobile, shown above. You could suspend any finished piece as a mobile, but it is better to mount the paper cutting first. This flattens the creases, protects the work, makes the mobile work better, and gives the work a finished look.

A disk or a polygon is a good shape for the main body of a mobile. They are among the simplest of wycinanki forms to make. You can create endless variations of lacelike designs in perfect symmetry by folding a circle in half three, four, or—for larger designs—even five times, depending on the paper thickness. The major element in the mobile pictured above was made from an 8-inch disk of gift-wrapping paper (red on one side, white on the other). It was folded four times. Other materials needed are 1 yard of 3-mil clear sheet vinyl (available at hardware stores), 1 yard of prefolded ¼-inch bias tape, and needle and thread. A sewing machine and iron are useful but not essential.

To make the mobile design shown, draw a circle at least 8 inches in diameter. Use a compass or trace around a dinner plate with a pencil. Cut out the circle and fold it in half (photograph 7). Crease the folded edge with your finger to make the paper lie flat. Fold the paper in half three more times to arrive at the pie-shaped wedge in photograph 8. With ruler and pencil, draw a light line from the tip of the wedge to the center of its curving edge; this will help keep the design centered.

The design I used is shown in Figure N. It contains a mixture of curved and straight cuts. If you like, sketch it lightly in pencil before you cut. Use small, sharp scissors to cut out the design; in a four-fold pattern, you will be working with 16 layers of paper. (To make a polygon rather than a circle, omit the cutouts on the curved edge of the wedge; instead cut straight across it to produce a triangle.) Unfold the paper carefully to avoid tearing it, and place it on a clean ironing board. Cover it with absorbent paper toweling and press it flat with a warm iron. You can also flatten the disk by weighting it for a few days.

If you want to add more color to your work, you can make an overlay in a circular, snowflake, or star motif (pages 2892 and 2893) to glue in the center of the disk with

N

Figure N: The cutting design used for the large disk in the mobile shown opposite needs its own center line to ensure symmetry (dashed line).

7: To begin cutting the design for the disk mobile shown opposite, cut out a paper circle at least 8 inches in diameter and fold it in half.

8: Fold the paper in half three more times to form the pie-shaped wedge shown; if the curved edge is squared off, the disk becomes a polygon.

9: Additional smaller paper cutouts can be added to the main design (with rubber cement) for extra color or to conceal imperfections.

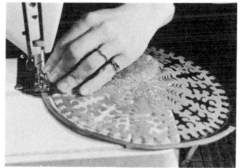

10: You can use a sewing machine to fasten bias tape to the edges of the paper disk after it has been covered with sheet vinyl.

rubber cement (photograph 9). This is also a good way to hide a mistake or an unsuccessful part of an otherwise satisfactory design.

To mount the flattened cutout, cut a double thickness of sheet vinyl 1½ inches larger in diameter than the disk. Place the wycinanki disk between the vinyl sheets. On the vinyl, outline the perimeter of the wycinanki with a ball-point pen. This mark, which you can later wipe away, will serve as a sewing guide. Machine- or hand-sew the vinyl sheets together, locking the paper cutout between them. Use a large stitch—eight stitches to the inch. Trim away any uneven areas on the border, but leave a ½-inch margin between the cutout and the edge of the vinyl. To make a decorative trim, fit the vinyl edges into a length of bias tape, and sew the tape to the vinyl (photograph 10). Hang the circle on a wire or thread. Add to it, if you like, smaller circles, stars, or crescents (made the same way) to complete the mobile.

Paper Folding and Cutting
Applied wycinanki

Wycinanki can be used in restoring old containers. A cookie tin and a file card box are rejuvenated with paper cutouts. A clear plastic finish makes the paper look inlaid.

New and interesting uses for wycinanki are not hard to devise. One practical project that I enjoy is using wycinanki to restore old containers to usefulness. An old cookie tin became the Valentine's Day present shown above, and an ordinary khaki-green box became a recipe file. The technique was the same in both instances, though the cookie tin was first painted with a glossy enamel.

For a result like the one on the cookie tin, you will need to make a heart-shaped tree-of-life cutout, a disk, and an accordion-fold cutout. To make the heart-shaped cutout and the disk, follow the instructions on pages 2895 through 2897. Let the heart be 4 inches narrower than the top of the tin and the disk ½ inch wider than the top. Cut the center out of the disk to leave room for the heart. To make the cutout that encircles the base of the box, follow the instructions on pages 2890 and 2891. The individual hearts in blue-green can be cut in multiple folds, for uniformity, then separated and inserted in every other heart cutout. Mount the work with liquid white glue. When it is dry, apply three coats of glossy acrylic medium, a clear plastic finish available at craft supply stores. The finish protects the paper and smooths the surface, so the wycinanki appears to be inlay work.

The file box was done the same way, except that all the scissor work was performed on accordion-folded paper.

For related projects and crafts, see "Découpage," "Greeting Cards," "Mobiles," "Origami," "Papermaking," "Silhouettes," "Stenciling," and "Valentines."

Other symmetrical wycinanki motifs you might incorporate in projects, include a multicolored flower (above), a circular crest with peacocks (top left), and a floral heart silhouette with cats (left).

YARD TOYS
Walk-In Playthings

Q. When is a doughnut like a trampoline?

A. When it is a giant inner tube lying flat on the ground.

A yard toy is not necessarily something manufactured to be a toy. Of course, you can always buy a set of swings and monkey bars. But as every child knows, the most unlikely objects can turn out to be a lot of fun to play with. Such objects are the basic building blocks of the yard toys pictured here. The materials are often given away or sold at low cost by utility companies, construction companies, and government agencies that deal in surplus. In the years that playgrounds have been my business, I have learned that fine designs can evolve from such recycled materials as old inner tubes, worn-out tires of every size, used utility poles, and empty cable spools. They should be carefully inspected for any hazards, of course; a splinter from an old pole or a pinch from a split tire is no fun. But with these basics and some caution, you can create the simple constructions shown on pages that follow; a child's imagination can turn them into a multitude of things. All of these toys except the inner tube require adult strength in the construction. But children can participate by offering suggestions and by supplying such finishing touches as paint and other trimmings.

Paul Hogan has helped to design and build play equipment in hundreds of communities. His book, Playgrounds for Free, *published by The MIT Press, describes how surplus materials can be used in creative playground construction. At his home in Phoenixville, Pennsylvania, a nonprofit corporation,* Playground Clearinghouse, Inc., *serves as a reference center for books, audio-visual materials, and ideas on the subject.*

Toys and Games
Inner-tube trampoline
¢ ⌛ 👥 🔥

Giant inner tubes that are 3 to 4 feet across when inflated are sometimes available free or at modest cost from transit companies. The one shown opposite and below is in my own yard. I always hear the gleeful giggles when the after-school crowd arrives. To inflate such a tube, take it to a gas station. Once the tube is inflated, be careful not to roll it over a sharp object. Two people can easily carry it home. Children never need instructions on how to bounce; they watch and learn from each other. Bouncing does require a bit of skill, of course, and there will be tumbles at first. To forestall injury, place the inflated tube on a soft bed of grass, pine needles, or tanbark for the young gymnasts to land on.

An oversized inner tube (opposite and above), resting on a soft cushion of grass, serves as a trampoline for active youngsters. The tube is 4 feet in diameter and was obtained from a transportation company.

A game of follow-the-leader takes on a new dimension when you are walking over stepping stones made from bouncy, partly buried tires.

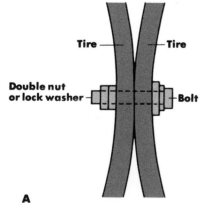

A
Figure A: To bolt two tires together, use two washers under the head of the bolt, placing one with a larger diameter against the rubber. This helps to prevent tearing. At the other end, tighten a lock washer and nut or a pair of nuts.

Toys and Games
Tire and box toys

The children shown above are lightly skipping over a line of bouncy stepping stones made of partially buried old tires. The easiest way to create such an unusual obstacle course is to dig a narrow trench half as deep as the diameter of the largest tire used. If you use tires of varying sizes, you will get an irregular up-and-down path. Before you sink the tires, drill a few holes for drainage through the part that will be buried. Set the tires in the trench and pack earth around the lower portions. Tamp the fill well, both inside and outside the tires, so it will not work loose. Set the tires so they don't become stumbling traps for the unwary; if there is a chance they will not be seen by a runner, paint the exposed tops a light color. Place the obstacle course out of the way of casual strollers.

Tire Cube
A cube made of old tires (opposite, top) keeps climbing close to the ground. Use six used tires about 2½ feet across. Four should be of identical size for use as the sides. A somewhat larger tire would give the cube a firm base. Bolt the tires to each other where they touch, using the hardware shown in Figure A. First bolt the side tires to the base; you may need a helping hand as you drill holes and insert bolts. Complete the cube by bolting on the top tire. Be sure to position the bolts where they will not project in such a way that they might cause injury; keep both ends inside the tires. Then let the children paint the cube with bright latex or oil paints, adding their own designs if they like. Drill drainage holes in the bottom of the base tire and fill it with earth or sand to make it absolutely stable.

Box Toys
Wooden packing crates make sturdy, if immobile, toy vehicles for small children. The one shown opposite is a plane that has tallied many air hours in the imaginations of young passengers and crew. It is made of a crate fitted with wings—a 2-by-12-inch plank placed across the top of the crate and nailed securely in place. The 2-by-4 supports nailed under the wings keep the plane from tipping sideways as passengers sit on the wings. Setting the crate up on cinder blocks is not essential, but it improves drainage to keep the wood from rotting. Be sure the points of all the crate nails or staples have been hammered flat so they do not stick out. Remove all wires or straps. Check for splintery edges and smooth any you find with coarse sandpaper or a wood rasp.

Above: A climbing cube made from surplus tires, bolted securely together, becomes a land of make-believe for preschoolers.

Below: Passengers and crew are ready for take-off in their make-believe plane assembled from a packing crate, cinder blocks, and a 2-by-12 wing.

Animals from utility poles

Old utility poles are useful in the construction of large toy animals like the giraffe pictured opposite. They are virtually indestructible.

Choosing the Poles
Used poles can sometimes be obtained free or at low cost from utility companies. New poles are undesirable in toys if they have been newly soaked in creosote, a toxic wood preservative that can burn hands and stain clothes. But old, dried-out poles are safe to use. The giraffe shown was made from one pole about 25 feet long and 8 inches in diameter; such a pole can be cut with a handsaw or a chain saw.

Either before or after you cut the pole into pieces, smooth off any rough spots with a rasp, a plane, or a drawknife. Then paint the pole with a coat of wood-softening chemical available at hardware stores. Parts that will be buried in the ground should be painted with fresh creosote to prevent rot.

Designing the Animal
A giraffe is appealing, but you may prefer to build a horse, a dog, or some other animal. Figure B is intended only as a guide to basic construction. Sketch your animal, deciding how much of the legs must be sunk in the ground. The length of the back leg projecting above the ground determines how high off the ground the animal's back will be. Small children use steps to mount the giraffe pictured, but the back can be as low as you like. Since the back crosspiece rests atop the back leg, it adds 8 inches to the height from the ground. If the back is very low, keep the rest of the animal in proportion. This giraffe's neck and front leg are long, over 17 feet, so this piece was sunk 4 feet into the ground. Shorter legs would need to be buried only 2 or 3 feet. In any case, the four basic pieces—front leg and neck, back, back leg, and head—are connected with ½-inch threaded rods hammered into drilled holes. Attach the head to the front leg and neck piece before it is put in the ground; otherwise, if the animal's head is high, you would need to climb a ladder to attach it.

Construction
To sink the legs you need holes that are deep and narrow. You can make such holes with a manual post-hole digger, a tool that can be rented. Cut the utility pole to the proper length, smooth it, and treat it with preservative; then dig the holes. If possible avoid sinking poles in ground that is heavy with clay; poor drainage will eventually cause rot.

Once the legs are in the ground, put the back piece on the back leg and hold it level while you mark where it meets the front leg. As shown in Figure B, notch the front end of the back piece and the neck so the two pieces fit snugly together. The notch can be cut with a handsaw.

Half-inch threaded steel rods, available at hardware stores, can be cut to 12- or 14-inch lengths with a hacksaw. These rods are used to join the pieces of the utility pole. Using a ½-inch bit with a 1-foot extension on a drill, bore through the joints at the places indicated in Figure B. Then hammer the rods into place. For safety, countersink the rod that joins the back to the back leg by drilling that hole ½ inch deeper than the length of the threaded rod. With the rod in place, fill the hole with a nonhardening silicone filler; this comes in a tube like caulking compound and should be used over any bolt heads, nuts, or rods that might project and cause injury.

Heads and Tails
Your animal should also have a tail, ears, eyes, mouth, and any other identifying characteristics. A tail can be fashioned with a large screw eye (4 inches long) and a length of frayed nylon or hemp rope. Insert the screw eye and tie on the rope. Insulator knobs can be used to make giraffe horns; pieces of rubber can be cut into ears and nailed on; 2-inch bumper reflectors make suitably wild eyes for any animal. If you want to add a halter, drill a hole larger than the thickness of your rope at the mouth and thread the halter through.

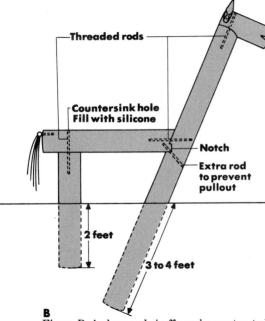

Threaded rods

**Countersink hole
Fill with silicone**

Notch

**Extra rod
to prevent
pullout**

2 feet

3 to 4 feet

B
Figure B: A play-yard giraffe can be constructed from four lengths cut from a utility pole. The pieces above ground are joined with threaded rods, hammered into drilled holes as shown.

A sturdy giraffe made of utility-pole sections has a back strong enough to carry several young riders at once. The parts are held together with threaded steel rods.

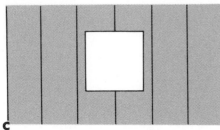

C
Figure C: To cut a window into the core of a cable spool, always cut partway across two slats. A single slat will fall out if it is cut through. Use a keyhole saw, starting it in holes drilled at each corner.

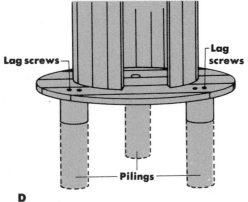

D
Figure D: For playhouse use, mount a cable spool on pilings—pieces of utility pole or railroad ties sunk in the ground—and secure the spool to the pilings with lag screws. This provides drainage beneath the spool and keeps it from being tipped on its side and rolled.

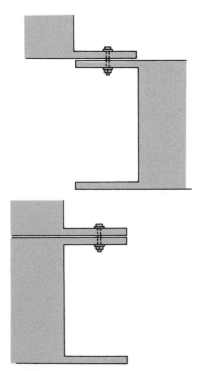

E
Figure E: When several cable spools are stacked or the edges overlapped to create a two-story playhouse, bolt the edges together, for safety.

Toys and Games
Cable-spool houses

A large, empty cable spool becomes a one-room playhouse once a door and a window are cut in the core. The spool is anchored to pilings sunk in the ground so it can't be tipped.

In rural areas, and sometimes in cities, cable spools are often discarded by companies that use cable. They can sometimes be obtained at construction sites. Empty cable spools can be turned into playhouses, either singly or clustered and bolted together as shown above and opposite. The larger the spool, the more spacious the play house. Beyond providing doors and windows, very little renovation has to be done.

To transport a large spool, you will need a truck and helpers. Once you have unloaded it, do not leave it unattended until it is fastened down. The spool seems to invite rolling and it is likely to be heavy enough to injure a child.

Construction
The core of a cable spool is made of slats that run between the circular sides. The interior of this core is reinforced with steel rods that act as braces between the sides. By removing two or three slats that fall between steel rods, you can make a door. Slats can be removed with a crowbar or hammer, but avoid hitting the steel rods.

To cut a window, cut only partway across each of two adjacent slats (Figure C). A slat will fall out if it is cut all the way across.

A castle results when several cable spools are assembled into a multi-room, multi-level play space. The wood is protected with bright house paints.

A spool house should be mounted on pilings and securely fastened down, not only for drainage but to keep it from being toppled (Figure D). The pilings can be 2-to-3-foot lengths cut from a utility pole or railroad tie and set vertically in the ground under the spool. Use at least three pilings per house. With the spool in place, drill through its base into the pilings and connect the two with 6-inch lag screws. Then the spool will be securely and permanently fastened down. Cover the ends of all protruding hardware with nonhardening silicone putty.

Cable-Spool Castles

A cable-spool castle, built from spools of varying sizes, is shown above. This is but one of an infinite number of cluster possibilities. The spool at the bottom left is secured to pilings in the manner described above. Smaller spools at the bottom center and right are fastened with lag screws to beams that are in turn fastened to pilings. And the top spools are screwed to those below. In this particular cluster, the ends of the spool do not overlap in a staggered pattern, but they could do so and be bolted together as shown in Figure E. Such a construction technique makes the structure very solid for climbers.

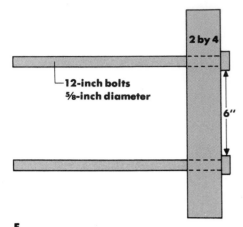

F
Figure F: To fasten a tire to a utility pole, first construct U-shaped units each with a 12-inch piece of 2-by-4 and two ⅝-inch bolts 12 inches long. Insert the bolts through the 2-by-4, then put the unit in a tire as shown in Figure G.

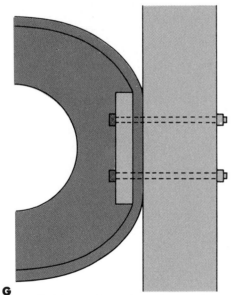

G
Figure G: After you insert the U-shaped unit inside the tire, push the bolts through the holes in the pole. Pull the tire against the pole and tighten the nuts. Then hammer the ends of the bolts so the nuts can't come off.

Figure H: A top view of the spiral staircase made with a utility pole and old tires shows how the tires are attached around the pole at intervals of 45 degrees. The bottom of the lowest tire is 12 inches from the ground. The pipe serves as a fireman's pole for sliding down while it anchors the utility pole solidly.

Toys and Games
Spiral staircase

One 10-foot utility pole, seven tires 2 feet in diameter, galvanized pipe, and some common hardware are needed to make the spiral staircase shown opposite. Youngsters enjoy ascending the squishy steps and sliding down the fire pole.

Drill all the needed holes through the pole while it is still lying on the ground. Drill two holes 6 inches apart vertically for each tire at 45-degree intervals around the pole, rising in 6-inch increments. (The lowest hole should be 18 inches from the ground.) As shown in the top view (Figure H), a pipe flange is attached in place of an eighth tire. Flatten a space for the flange with a hatchet or rasp; then attach it with lag screws. Use a post-hole digger and sink the utility pole at least 4 feet into the ground. Such a pole is heavy; you will need several adults to erect it. Attach a short length of pipe to the flange and attach a 90-degree elbow at the outer end. Directly below the elbow, dig a hole 8 inches in diameter and 2 or 3 feet deep using a post-hole digger. This will be about 2½ feet from the pole. Attach the long pipe to the elbow, positioning the free end in the hole. Fill the hole with ready-mix concrete, adding some rocks and chunks of brick. Let the concrete harden for at least 12 hours.

Tire Assembly
For each tire you will need a 1-foot length of 2-by-4, two ⅝-inch bolts 10 inches long, and two nuts (Figure F). As shown in Figure G, the 2-by-4 acts as a giant washer inside the tire to keep the rubber from ripping. First make all the U-shaped assemblies with bolts and 2-by-4s. Drill two holes 6 inches apart in each tire and insert the U-shaped assembly with the 2-by-4 inside the tire. Push the bolts through the holes drilled in the pole, and screw the nuts on the ends, tightening them with a wrench.

If more than ¼ inch of bolt protrudes beyond the other nut, cut it off with a hacksaw to ¼ inch. Then hammer the end of each bolt to round it off so the nuts can't come loose. Apply a glob of outdoor nonhardening silicone on the ends of the bolts to cover all sharp edges. Drill a few holes in the bottom of each tire so rainwater will not collect inside.

For related entries, see "Plastic Pipe Constructions," "Swings," and "Tree Houses."

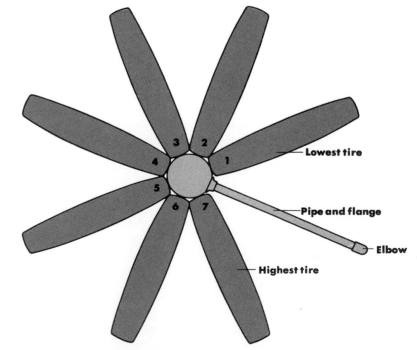

H

The tires make an "up" staircase; to get back down, the climber wraps himself around the fire pole and slides.

Ramón Medina Silva, a Huichol Indian artist, created this yarn painting to record a legend concerning the origin of maize. In ancient times, the Huichols had no maize, so a young boy went over the mountains in search of it. On the way he met and joined a group of ant men (the insects in the picture), not knowing they stole by nibbling anything they could find. The boy awoke under a great pine tree to find his clothes and hair nibbled away, and only his bow and arrows left. When he heard a bird land in the tree, he aimed an arrow at it. But the bird spoke, revealing that she was *Tatéi Kukurú Uimári*, Our Mother Dove Girl, and the mother of maize. She told him to follow her and she would give him maize.

YARN PAINTING

Coloring with Fiber

Creating a picture with colorful yarns instead of paints is fun, but to the Huichol Indians of West-Central Mexico, yarn paintings can have religious significance.

The Huichols, whose religious art also includes *ojo de dios* yarn sculptures, make these sacred art objects as offerings to their divine beings, the gods of nature. There is no word for God in the Huichol language; the people call their divine beings by kinship terms, such as Our Grandfather or Our Mother Eagle Girl. Objects used in the worship of these divinities have traditionally been called *nearikas*. A *nearika* can be as simple as a few scratches in a disk of volcanic ash or as complex as a grouping of beeswax effigies embellished with yarn, seeds, and beads. At one time, yarn paintings were considered strictly a folk art by the Huichols, but they have become the newest form of *nearika*.

Yarn paintings with religious significance differ from those that are simply folk art. The primary difference is the intention of the artist, but variations in form and material also distinguish the two. Ceremonial yarn paintings are made on a wood backing and have rounded corners; folk-art panels made for sale are backed with composition board and may have sharp corners. Motifs of both are taken from Huichol history, religion, and visions. They include representations of animals, people, and divine beings. In folk-art yarn paintings, such symbols are usually placed in a meaningless (though visually interesting) arrangement. But the symbols of a ceremonial panel are chosen to pertain only to the divine being for whom the *nearika* is intended. The color choice is arbitrary except for certain sacred subjects, although bright colors are usually preferred because they seem more visionary.

Patricia Lee is a production artist and designer for a New York book publisher. Her interests include photography and all types of graphic arts and needlecrafts. She is pictured with her niece, Donna Lynn Chin, who made two of the yarn paintings shown on pages that follow.

Yarn Painting as a Modern Craft

As a base for the yarn, the Huichols use a special wax found in the High Sierras. For use, it is mixed with resin and softened by the sun, never heated over a fire. If you want to try yarn painting, you can use a mixture of batik wax and petroleum jelly, heated in the top of a double boiler. White household glue is recommended for projects done by children and as a base for rough, stiff cords.

The yarn the Huichols use is a solid-color wool with a slight twist to it. You can use either wool or synthetic yarn. Wool, however, gives better texture and tends to expand, filling empty spaces. Recommended are knitting worsted, rug yarn, and novelty yarns with interesting textures or color mixes. Macramé cords, string, and jute can be introduced for more variety. Feathers, beads, and other trimmings can also be incorporated.

Traditional yarn paintings are backed with wood or composition board, but you can also create such yarn paintings on paper, cardboard, illustration board, or plastic. You can even work in three dimensions by covering a bottle, can, cup, or box with yarn.

Yarn Painting Techniques

For projects in which glue is used, draw or trace the pattern onto the cardboard or other backing with pencil or felt-tipped marker. Errors will be hidden by the yarn. Apply glue in thin lines; then press the yarn into the glue and hold it with your fingers until the glue sets. Apply small amounts of glue at one time so it does not dry too quickly. Press the yarn down gently so the glue does not stain yarn that will show.

To make a wax base, put 4 ounces of batik wax and ¼ ounce of petroleum jelly in the top of a double boiler. Melt the mixture over boiling water. Never melt the wax directly over a heat source lest it catch fire. Stir until the petroleum jelly is completely dissolved in melted wax. Allow the mixture to cool in the pot, or pour it into a small cake pan or crockery dish for cooling.

The best results are achieved with this wax when the air temperature is near 75 degrees Fahrenheit. If the wax has cooled to the point where it is hard, put it in the sun or near heat until it begins to soften. Then pry it out with a spoon and knead it into several fist-sized balls. When you have kneaded the wax to a workable consistency, break off a small piece and use your thumb to press it hard onto the backing board. Spread the wax about ½ inch thick, being sure not to skimp on the edges. It should look like cool butter after it is spread. Before you cover the entire backing, experiment with the yarn or yarns you plan to use. If the layer of wax is too thin, the yarn will not hold well; but if it is too thick, the yarn may sink too deep into it.

Sketch the design into the wax with a stylus or other pointed instrument; any error can easily be removed by smoothing the wax with your fingers.

You may want to follow tradition and outline the entire picture with several rows of yarn. This is usually done with alternating colors. To begin and end the yarn lengths neatly, cut them straight across and twist each strand tightly before you press it into the wax. Careful placement of the first strand is important; all the others will follow it. It is a good idea to outline all the individual shapes of the painting before you start to fill any one, so you can see them in relation to each other and make changes if they are needed. This is especially true when you work with wax because the outlines will not be as pronounced as those drawn with a pencil or felt-tipped marker. Using your thumbnail, press the yarn about ⅛ inch into the wax or glue. Hold the yarn taut with one hand as you position it with the other. Be sure the yarn is holding well before you proceed.

You can fill in the shapes with parallel rows, spirals, or any yarn configuration that covers the space. In each shape, use one continuous strand of yarn. You can start at the center and work out or at the edge and work inward. To make parallel rows, bend the yarn back on itself. Pinch the corners to make them sharp and definite; they will tend to round naturally. Place each strand of yarn as close as possible to the previous strand. (The Huichols often work with several strands at one time, but this takes practice.) Cut the yarn wherever necessary; never overlap two strands. At the end of each strand, again twist the ends and press the yarn into the wax. Large areas of solid color such as a background should be filled in last. Cover these large areas with small, mosaiclike sections to create changes of texture where there is no change of color.

No two yarn paintings will ever be alike, so it is not necessary to follow the project instructions exactly. Just remember the basic rule: fill in each open area with a continuous strand of yarn; then start a new area.

Designs and Decorations
Portrait of a clown

For her first yarn painting, Donna chose to make the clown's face shown opposite, and I guided her, step by step. You can work with a child in the same way. First, draw a bold outline of the subject on a piece of heavy cardboard or illustration board (photograph 1). Coloring books are a good source of designs. Keep the areas to be filled with yarn large and uncomplicated. Sketch the design with pencil; then go over the lines with a felt-tipped marker. All the lines will be hidden by yarn. With a little help, the child can do the rest. Thick yarn—quick-point, bulky weight, or rug yarn—is easiest for little fingers to handle. Clear-drying white liquid glue in a squeeze bottle is the neatest adhesive to use.

For young artists, it is best to start the yarn in the center of the board; then work out to the edges. Donna started with the clown's nose, covering the circle with glue and spiraling a length of red yarn from the edge of the circle toward the middle. At the center she cut the yarn straight across and tightly twisted the end before pressing it into the glue. Then she held the entire section in place until the glue had set.

Next, she applied glue to the line of the clown's mouth and pressed a double row of red yarn into it (photograph 2). She then squeezed more glue onto the surrounding area and applied the yellow yarn, starting next to the red yarn and gradually working outward (photographs 3 and 4). The eyes, indicated on the drawing by Xs, came next. Each eye has one short piece of yarn crossing another, thus breaking the rule against overlapping yarn. (Such layering gives dimension to the eyes and, for a child, is easier than joining four tiny pieces.) The double thickness makes it

1: To help a child start a yarn painting, sketch a design with pencil; then outline the final sketch with a felt-tipped marker. The heavy lines will be hidden by yarn.

2: Let the child fill in the design. Here, Donna gives the clown a double row of red yarn for his smile; she has already finished the red nose.

3: Once the shape is established, the child can outline it with glue for more yarn.

4: After each row of yarn is applied, Donna presses it firmly into the glue so it will stick.

Since the circus is one of Donna's favorite entertainments, she chose to make a clown's face in her first yarn painting project.

5: Two pieces of yarn are crossed to make each eye. Extra glue may be needed where they cross to hold them securely.

6: The clown's triangular hat is covered with glue, then outlined and filled in with a single length of yarn.

7: Finally, the clown's ruff and hair are covered. Both are curved and scalloped at the edges.

essential that the yarn be firmly pressed into the glue and held there until the glue sets (photograph 5). You may have to add an extra drop of glue where the yarn lengths cross.

The next area filled was the hat. Donna put glue over the entire triangle before she pressed the yarn in place. The first row was applied around the outside edge and each of the others was pressed down as close as possible to the preceding row (photograph 6). After making the pompon atop the clown's hat (another spiral), Donna filled in his ruff and hair with a textured, scalloped effect (photograph 7).

After all of your design is filled, cover the background by using the same techniques. Divide large areas into smaller ones to add textural interest. Let the glue dry before hanging the finished yarn painting.

Designs and Decorations
Paper-plate mask

Even shy children lose inhibitions when they hide behind a mask. This yarn-painting mask, based on a paper plate, is fun for young children to make as well as to play with.

Paper plates can be cut into masks and covered with yarn—a good rainy-day project. A child can apply the glue and yarn, then play "let's pretend" as he hides behind the finished work, as shown opposite.

Cut the holes for the eyes, nose, and mouth first; then let the child create a fantasy face with brightly colored yarns. You may want to place the first rows around the cutouts; otherwise, leave the placement of the yarn up to the imagination of the young artist.

Designs and Decorations
Starry-night landscape

Although the yarn painting of a starry night shown below is more sophisticated than the children's projects, it is also held with glue rather than wax because the material used is roughly textured jute, and glue holds it more securely.

Draw the basic outlines of the trees, the moon, and the rolling hills on a piece of illustration board. (The landscape shown is 12 inches square.) Outline each shape with jute; then fill it in, paying attention to the textural patterns achieved as well as the colors. For the tree trunks, apply the jute vertically; for the tree tops, make irregularly curved shapes. In the landscape shown, the moon is the only part done with soft, bulky yarn instead of jute; it is a simple spiral. Texture alone defines the hills in the foreground. The deep-blue jute of the sky swirls about in random patterns with a tiny sequin centered in each swirl.

This yarn painting was created largely with jute, a rough, ropelike cord that is often used for macramé. It is held in place with white glue. Tiny sequins light up the night sky.

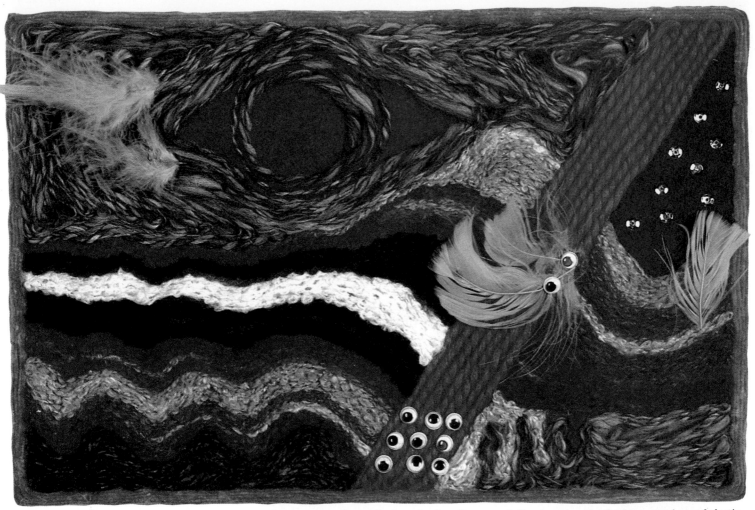

This landscape abstraction is a mixed-media yarn painting, incorporating feathers, sequins, and plastic eyes as well as yarn and jute.

8: The yarns used in the abstract landscape above are blue polyester-and-wool tweed, an acrylic yarn with nine colors in one ball, orange velvet-textured needlepoint yarn, green jute, pink quick-point yarn, and scraps of red and blue knitting worsted.

Designs and Decorations
Landscape with feathers

The landscape shown above is a mixed-media yarn painting. It combines several yarns of varying textures and colors with feathers, sequins, and small, plastic roll-about eyes. However, it is worked in a traditional way on composition board with wax as the adhesive.

Cut a piece of composition board the size desired (the landscape shown is 8 by 12 inches). Then prepare a mixture of batik wax and petroleum jelly (page 2911). Spread this wax over the face of the board (photograph 9).

Outline the perimeter of the board with three rows of yarn (I used a velvet-textured needlepoint yarn for this). You can scratch a rough pattern in the wax with a stylus or create free-form designs without an outline to follow, mixing the yarns in a spontaneous way. Do not cut the yarn until you have finished a section, and pinch the yarn where it must turn back on itself.

An interesting effect can be created by using an ombre yarn (shaded from dark to light) or a multicolor yarn. The area at the lower left of the landscape, above the green jute and below the blue tweed sky, was made with only one yarn, a yarn with nine coordinated colors in it. I pressed this yarn into the wax in a scalloped pattern (photograph 10). If a novelty-textured yarn like this doesn't stick easily in the wax, you may have to place the board in the sun or near a heat source to soften the wax a bit. Be careful not to heat it so much that the yarn sinks into the wax.

9: To form a wax base for a yarn painting, use your thumb to spread a ½-inch-thick layer over the backing material.

10: Press the yarn firmly into the wax as you work. This is especially important with a novelty-textured yarn.

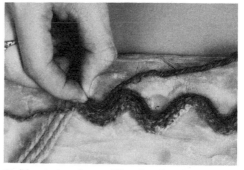

11: If you are using a stiff cord such as jute, pinch the corners tightly at the end of each row that doubles back.

Stiff jute does not adhere as well to wax as it does to glue. I used it in only a small area, pinching the corners tightly at the end of each row (photograph 11). As I reached the bottom of the board, I cut short pieces of jute and bent them to fit into the spaces left between the last row and the edge of the board (photograph 12).

Glue the feathers and other trimmings on top of the yarn.

12: To fill in gaps left by curved rows, cut short pieces of the same yarn and bend them to fit.

Designs and Decorations
Shampoo-bottle yarn painting ¢ ⌛ ♦ 🧵

With yarn painting, an empty plastic shampoo bottle, destined for the wastebasket, can be salvaged and turned into a decorative accessory for bedroom or bathroom. For the one shown below, a traditional wax base was used.

Wash the bottle thoroughly and let it dry. Then mix batik wax and petroleum jelly, (page 2911) and spread the mixture over the outside of the bottle and the cap. Glue will not hold yarn to plastic. Use the techniques described for flat yarn paintings, outlining the basic shapes first, then filling them in with yarn.

This bottle has a heart on one side and a teardrop on the other. If you choose another motif, keep it simple; there is little room for details on a small object.

For related projects, see "Masks" and "Ojo de Dios."

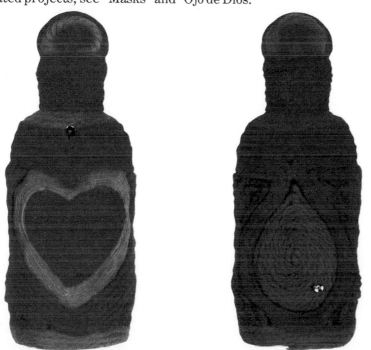

A three-dimensional yarn painting results when a bottle or box is covered. One side of this plastic shampoo bottle has a heart on it (left), the other has a teardrop, glistening with a sequin (right).

Toys with Ups and Downs

Bruce Michel (left), who designed the three homemade yo-yos on these pages, has built, repaired, and taken apart mechanical devices from kaleidoscopes to sailboats.

Rodney Friedman (right), who demonstrates yo-yo tricks on these pages, was a yoyophile at the age of five. By age ten, he had abandoned the yo-yo in favor of football, baseball, basketball, and lacrosse. Many bruises later, he returned to yo-yoing with an appreciation of its nonviolent nature.

The toy called a yo-yo (or return top) originated as a primitive weapon in the jungles of the Philippine Islands. The weapon was fashioned from a sharp rock tied to a long thong of leather or plant fiber. The attacker would hide in a tree and wait for his prey to pass underneath. Then he would throw the stone, trying to stun the prey. If he missed, he could retrieve the rock by means of the thong.

While the yo-yo has changed from weapon to toy, it has remained popular in the Philippines. Doing tricks with a yo-yo is a national sport there. Many Filipinos make their own intricately carved yo-yos of wood or horn.

The yo-yo was also popular in the courts of France and Spain during the seventeenth and eighteenth centuries; a painting of a nobleman of that time, holding a yo-yo, is in the Louvre. The French named the yo-yo *l'emigrette;* the English knew it by the names *incroyable, bandalore,* or *quiz.*

In the late 1920s, the toy first became known as a yo-yo. Donald F. Duncan promoted the Duncan yo-yo in America, and it remained a family business until 1968, when ownership was acquired by the Flambeau Plastics Corporation. A team of Duncan Champions still tours the country, performing tricks, showing boys and girls how to operate a yo-yo, and conducting contests.

Yo-yo Competitions

Uniform procedures have been developed for conducting a yo-yo contest, based on ten tricks known as: the spinner, walk-the-dog, the creeper, three-leaf clover, loop-the-loop, around-the-corner, skin-the-cat, sleeping beauty, rock-the-baby, and the-man-on-the-flying-trapeze. These tricks are demonstrated or illustrated on pages 2922 through 2925.

Each contestant has two tries for each trick. Ten points are awarded if the trick is done on the first try, five if on the second. At the conclusion of each trick, the yo-yo must be back in hand, with all string wound. (If the string breaks, an extra try is allowed without penalty.)

In the event of a tie, the top contenders resort to tie-breaking tricks, such as each performing loop-the-loop as many times as he or she can.

Toys and Games

Drawer-pull yo-yo

Opposite: It takes patience and practice to learn to do tricks with a yo-yo, but once you've mastered several, you can delight your friends as you entertain yourself. Here, a trick known as loop-the-loop (page 2923) is performed.

Right: A workable yo-yo can be made from two wooden drawer pulls and a short length of doweling. The bull's-eye design was painted on the pulls, following the pattern of the grooves.

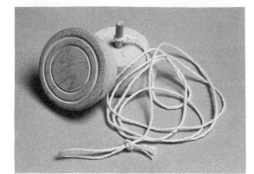

1: Two flush-type wooden drawer pulls can be connected with a short dowel. Inserted in the screw holes, it will be precisely centered.

2: A kitchen-sink strainer (above, right) can be disassembled into three pieces: a connector (left) that you discard, a rubber disk, and a perforated metal bowl. Two strainers provide matching parts for two yo-yos.

3: The two rubber disks can be joined with a short piece of dowel to make a yo-yo small enough to carry in a shirt pocket.

A yo-yo that is easy to make and works surprisingly well consists of a pair of wooden drawer pulls connected with a short dowel (photograph 1). The pulls are predrilled, sparing you the problem of finding the exact centers. (Finding the exact centers is crucial because a yo-yo must be balanced to function properly.)

The drawer pulls used for the yo-yo shown are flat-backed and measure 2 inches in diameter and 7/8 inch in depth. The diameter of the dowel needed should match the screw holes in the pulls you select.

Glue the dowel in place with white glue so there is ⅛ inch between the pulls. Use the glue sparingly; any excess would interfere with the smooth movement of the string. Paint the pulls with enamel or acrylic paint. A commercial twisted yo-yo string that will let the yo-yo spin freely is best; these are available at larger variety stores. (For the proper way to string a yo-yo, see Craftnotes opposite).

Toys and Games
Sink-strainer yo-yos

Two kitchen-sink strainers from the hardware store provide the parts to make two yo-yos. The larger is made with two metal strainer bowls and a bolt; the smaller consists of two rubber disks held together with a dowel. The twisted yo-yo strings are commercial products.

Two yo-yos can be made from two kitchen sink strainers, available in hardware stores. Each strainer includes a perforated metal bowl, a rubber disk, and a connector (photograph 2).

For one yo-yo, connect the two metal bowls, back to back, with a large bolt and a matching nut. (The diameter and length of the bolt will vary with the size of the strainers.) I leave a small space between the two bowls for the string. (With this yo-yo, you will not be able to do the spinner shown on page 2922, but you will be able to do other tricks that do not involve spinning.)

To make the second yo-yo, small enough to fit in a shirt pocket, hold the two rubber disks with the flat sides together, and push a 1-inch length of ¼-inch dowel through the center holes (photograph 3). Slip a commercial yo-yo string around the dowel.

CRAFTNOTES: YO-YO BASICS

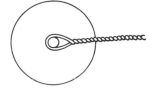

Attaching the string
To put a commercial string on a yo-yo, un-twist the end loop until it is large enough to slip over the yo-yo and into the center slot. Do not twist the string tightly around the axle—there should be some space in the loop so the yo-yo can spin freely at the end of the string.

Finger loop
To make a finger loop on the free end of the string, make a slip knot by tying a loop and pulling part of the long end of the string through it.

Rewinding the string
To rewind a yo-yo when the string has become unwound or tangles, let the yo-yo hang at the end of its string until it stops spinning. Hold the yo-yo in your free hand with your thumb on top, keeping the string taut. Give the yo-yo a strong flick with your thumb and the yo-yo will climb the string.

Determining the length
Be sure the yo-yo string is the right length for you. It should reach your waistline when the yo-yo is touching the floor and the string is pulled taut.

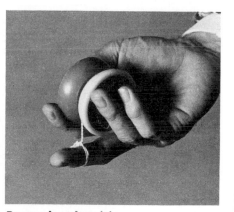

Proper hand position
With the slip knot over your middle finger and the yo-yo in your palm with the string coming off its top, you are ready to try a trick.

Ten Basic Tournament Tricks

The Spinner (also called Sleeping)

1. This is a trick you should learn to do well since it is the basis for many other tricks. (To make the yo-yo spin as long as possible, rub a little candle wax on 4 inches of the string, working down from the finger loop. This gives added momentum to the start of the spin.) First, toss the yo-yo forward and down with a flick of the wrist.

2. When the yo-yo reaches the end of the string, let it hang, spinning. (Your hand will be turned palm up.) But just before it stops spinning, give the string an easy tug and turn your hand palm down; the yo-yo will climb the string to return to your hand.

Walking-the-Dog

1. To begin this trick, throw a fast spinner; then very gently lower your hand so the yo-yo is on the floor.

2. Let the yo-yo roll forward for a short distance. Do not allow any slack in the string. A slight tug on the string will return the yo-yo to your hand.

Skin-the-Cat

1. Throw a fast spinner, and slide the first finger of your free hand under the string so it touches the finger holding the yo-yo string.

2. Pull back on the string with your other hand.

3. Stop pulling when the yo-yo is several inches away from your free hand.

4. Gently flip up the yo-yo so it makes a loop and returns to your hand.

The Creeper

1. Throw a fast spinner, and gently lower the yo-yo to the floor by bending your body until your hand is just a few inches from the floor.

2. Let the yo-yo roll forward on the floor until it reaches the end of its string. Tug quickly on the string at this point, and the yo-yo will bounce back along the floor and into your hand.

Rocking-the-Baby

Practice this first without spinning the yo-yo. Let it hang the full length of the string.

1. With your free hand, reach over and pass the string across the back of your fingers.

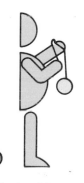

2. Drop your other hand down to catch the string about 4 inches from the yo-yo. This forms a triangle.

3. Drop your free hand down to turn the triangle over and swing the yo-yo back and forth through the triangle.

Once you have practiced the maneuver, try it while doing a fast spinner. To make the yo-yo return to your hand, flick it out of the triangle, and catch it when it pops back to you.

Sleeping Beauty

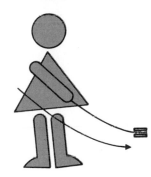

1. Start this trick by holding your arm with the elbow bent, and snap the yo-yo down and sideways so it crosses your body diagonally.

2. The yo-yo will spin on its side; lift it by catching the string with your free hand about 12 inches from the yo-yo.

3. The yo-yo will return to your hand if you let go of the string near the yo-yo, and, at the same time, give it a quick tug at the finger loop. (Throwing the yo-yo to the left untwists the string; to the right tightens it.)

Loop-the-Loop

1. Snap the yo-yo out in front of you, but do not catch it when it returns to you.

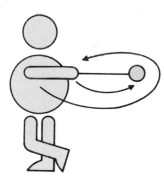

2. Instead, bend your wrist sharply in a circular motion so the yo-yo will loop around your hand and take off again. To avoid hitting yourself with the yo-yo, keep your arm stretched out in front of you as you make the loop.

Around-the-Corner

1. Throw a fast spinner; then bend your elbow and move your hand up and back so the yo-yo is dangling from the string behind you.

2. Tug on the string, and the yo-yo will climb the string and roll over your shoulder.

3. Let the yo-yo drop in front of you, and it will roll up into your hand.

Man-on-the-Flying-Trapeze

1. Start by tossing the yo-yo out and across your body.

2. With the first finger of your free hand, loop the string several inches from the yo-yo.

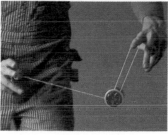

3. Let the yo-yo land on the string behind the loop and ride along the string, still spinning.

4. As you move the finger of your free hand, the yo-yo will go back and forth. To return the yo-yo to your hand, give it a quick flip with both hands at the same time you slip your free hand from the loop.

Three-Leaf Clover

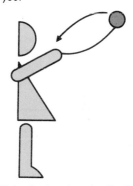

1. Snap the yo-yo out in front of of you.

2. Make the first cloverleaf by throwing a high loop.

3. As the yo-yo comes back to you, snap your wrist and send it straight out in front of you to make the second leaf.

4. Then make a low loop and let the yo-yo return to your hand to complete the three-leaf clover.

For related projects, see "Spool Toys," and "Toys."

ZOETROPE TOYS
Pictures in Motion

Spin a coin on its edge and it may seem that you can see both sides at once. This happens because for a brief moment, the eye retains an after image of anything it has seen, so it superimposes any two images viewed in rapid succession. This phenomenon, known as the persistence of vision or the formation of positive after-images, had been known for centuries. But it wasn't until the beginning of the nineteenth century that this optical illusion was used to make a series of pictures appear to move. The simplest animation device is a flip disk or card, called a thaumatrope, which has one image on one side and a complementary image on the other. The eye perceives the two images as one as the device spins. This led to devices that could make drawn figures appear to be alive and moving. The praxinoscope shown opposite is one such device. It consists of a drum lined with images and a mirror-covered center column. As this drum is spun, the images seem to merge—and move.

Optical Toys

Many of the picture-manipulating devices that were developed for scientific research were later simplified and mass-produced as toys. Only a handful of these survive in museums and private collections. But they are easy to make using household materials, such as scissors, white glue, and index cards. If you have access to a copying machine, you can quickly reproduce the patterns shown here. Projects that follow include simple thaumatropes (below) and movie wheels (page 2930), both good projects for children. Somewhat more advanced is the zoetrope—a movie drum—on page 2934, and the kineograph—a book that turns into a movie as its pages are flipped (page 2942).

One hundred years ago, no one had ever seen an animated cartoon, much less a full-length feature film. These toys were the forerunners of present-day cinema.

Martin Abrahams was born in Brooklyn, New York. As a child he acted in movies, then studied painting. In California he worked as a production assistant for master filmmaker Michelangelo Antonioni. He returned to New York to make animated films, produce children's television programs, and teach animation at the School of Visual Arts.

Paper Cutting and Folding
Thaumatropes   ¢ ⧗ 👥 🧯

The thaumatrope, about as simple as an optical toy can be, was invented in 1825 by an Englishman, Dr. John Ayrton Paris. Its small disk or card has images on both sides. As the device is spun, the images seem to form a single picture.

To see the rocket ship appear in a dark, star-studded sky, the girl at right rolled the pencil shaft between her palms, spinning it quickly to make the images seem to be one. By rolling the elastic bands at each side of a thaumatrope between thumb and forefinger, the boy at left made the disk spin over and over. The faster the disk moved, the easier it was for him to see the superimposed images as a single picture.

Left: If you spin the outer drum, the lady reflected in the center mirrors will appear to flip an omelet. This gadget, the praxinoscope, was patented by a French artist, Emile Reynaud, in 1877. This is one of the pre-cinema inventions in the collection of Alan and Hilary Weiner, New York.

Many early thaumatropes were designed to portray figures in motion. This pattern appeared in Volume 4 of *The Boy's Own Annual*, published in 1881. When the horse and rider patterns were pasted back to back and the disk was spun, the man appeared to be thrown from the horse.

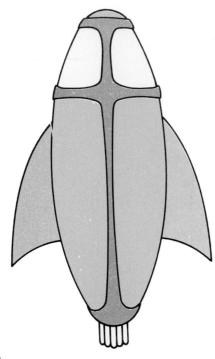

A

Figure A: For the thaumatrope shown on page 2927, copy this full-sized rocket ship pattern onto tracing paper; then use carbon paper to transfer it to an index card.

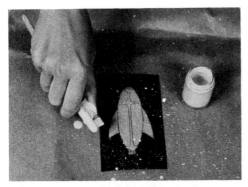

1: To paint a starry background for the thaumatrope rocket, tape a tracing of the rocket to the black side of a card and put the card on a newspaper. Dip an old toothbrush in diluted white poster paint and spatter it on the card by running your thumb over the bristles.

2: To make a handle, tape a pencil near the bottom of the rocket card. Then glue the star card, face up, over the pencil.

A Card Thaumatrope

To make the thaumatrope held by the girl on page 2927, you need to join two images, back to back, one showing a rocket and the other a starry sky. You will need: a pencil; 8-by-10-inch sheets (one each) of tracing paper, carbon paper, and black construction paper; scissors; ruler; three 3-by-5-inch index cards; rubber cement; masking tape; an old toothbrush; and a small jar of white poster paint.

Trace the rocket pattern (Figure A). Use carbon paper to transfer the tracing to an index card; then cut out the rocket from both tracing paper and index card.

Glue a 3-by-5-inch piece of black construction paper to one side of each remaining index card. Glue the index-card rocket to the black face of one card. Color the rocket with crayons or felt-tipped markers. Lightly tape the rocket tracing to the other black card. (The two rockets must be in identical positions on the cards.) Decorate the background of the second card with star shapes by spattering white poster paint around the tracing with an old toothbrush (photograph 1).

To assemble the thaumatrope, tape a pencil to the inside bottom of one card (photograph 2). Making sure both rockets point in the same direction, use rubber cement to join the cards, back to back, with the pencil between them. When the cement is dry, remove the rocket tracing. Then test the illusion by rolling the projecting pencil between your palms. If you move the cards smoothly and rapidly, the pictures will seem to merge so the rocket appears to be zooming through the sky.

Disk Thaumatropes

The thaumatrope shown being spun by the boy on page 2927 incorporates the patterns in Figure B. When they are glued together, back to back, and the disk is spun, the face (my version of a Martian) appears in the porthole of the spaceship. Such disks work on the same principle as a thaumatrope card with one exception. Because the disk rotates horizontally, the upside-down image on the back is right side up when it comes to the front. So when the thaumatrope is assembled, one image must be upside down for the illusion to work.

To make this thaumatrope, you will need: one 9-by-12-inch sheet each of tracing paper, carbon paper, and blue construction paper; three 5-by-7-inch index cards; pencil; masking tape; drafting compass; scissors; rubber cement; paper punch; two thin rubber bands; an old toothbrush; yellow poster paint; and felt-tipped markers or crayons.

To begin, scribe and cut two 4-inch circles from index cards and two from blue construction paper. Glue a blue circle on each index-card circle. Trace the rocket and Martian face patterns (Figure B). Transfer them to the third index card with carbon paper; then cut them out. Spatter-paint the blue disk that will be behind the rocket ship to get yellow star shapes. When the paint is dry, glue the index-card rocket ship to the painted blue disk and the Martian to the other blue disk. Position them as shown in Figure B. When the glue is dry, color the designs with felt-tipped markers or crayons.

In assembly, the rocket must be right side up and the Martian upside down. Glue the disks together that way, back to back. When the rubber cement is dry, punch a hole on each side of the disk, ¼ inch in from its edge.

Insert one end of a rubber band through each hole, and loop it through itself to hold it.

To make the images on each side of the disk merge into one picture, spin the disk as smoothly and rapidly as possible. To do this, hold the free end of each elastic band between a thumb and forefinger. Gently spin the elastic as you watch the disk. The Martian's face will appear to be at the porthole of the rocket ship.

Designing Your Own Thaumatropes

You will find it easy to design other thaumatropes. In Figure C, for example, is a photograph of an arm and outstretched hand for one side of a disk, an upside-down drawing of a bug for the other side. As the disk rotates, the bug will appear to rest in the hand.

If you design your own thaumatrope, remember that a white or bright-colored image on one side will stand out best against a dark or complementary colored image on the other. To position images, hold them back to back over a flashlight or in front of a window so you can see through both pieces of paper.

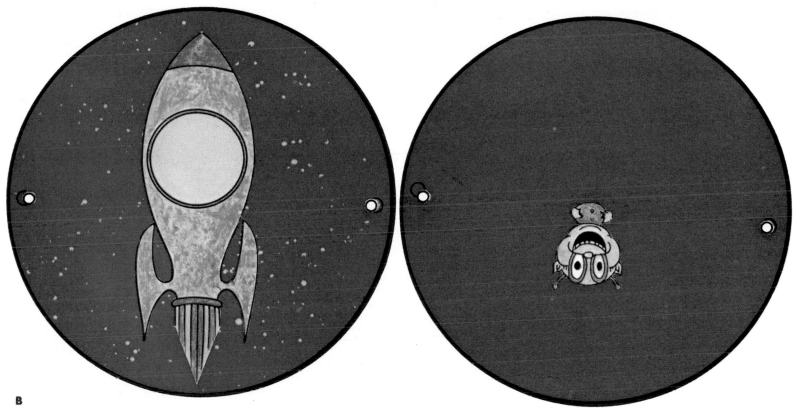

B

Figure B: These thaumatrope patterns for the disk shown on page 2927 can be copied onto tracing paper, then transferred to an index card with carbon paper.

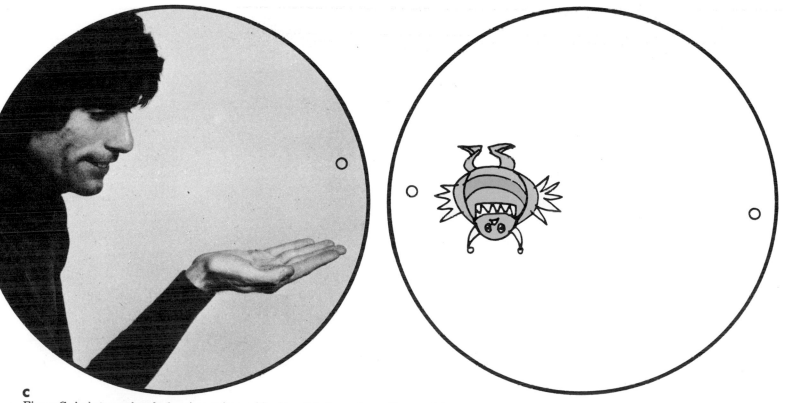

C

Figure C: A photograph and a drawing can be combined in a disk thaumatrope. If you prefer, you can trace the outline of the man pictured or use a magazine picture in place of a photograph.

Bibliography

Animated Cartoons by E.G. Lutz. Charles Scribner's Sons, New York, New York.

Animated Film Concept Methods and Uses by Roy Madsen. Interland Publishing Inc., New York, New York.

Animation Nos. 25 and 26 by Preston Blair.

Archaeology of the Cinema by C.W. Ceram. Harcourt, Brace and World, New York, New York.

Catalog of Fine Antique Cameras and Photographic Images No. 7 by Alan and Hilary Weiner. Weiner, New York, New York.

How to Make Animated Movies by Anthony Kinsey. The Viking Press, New York, New York.

Movement in Two Dimensions by Olive Cook. Hutchinson and Co., Ltd., London, England.

Origins of Motion Pictures by D.B. Thomas. Her Majesty's Stationery Office, London, England.

Paper Movie Machines by Budd Wentz. Troubadour Press, San Francisco, California.

Techniques of Film Animation by John Halas and Roger Manvell. Hastings House Publishers Inc., New York, New York.

Paper Folding and Cutting
Moving-picture wheels

In 1832 two inventors created similar devices for producing moving pictures. Joseph Plateau of Belgium called his a phenakistoscope and Simon Ritter von Stampfer of Austria named his a stroboscope. Each contrivance consisted of a disk covered with evenly spaced pictures of a figure, such as the circus acrobat shown below. When the disk was spun, the after image permitted the eye to blend the images in the separate pictures so the figure portrayed appeared to move. For the sequence of images, the figure was drawn in each of a series of sequential postures representing a movement. Each picture could be only slightly different from the last. Then, for the eye to perceive motion, it had to be able to view only one picture

Picture wheels were a popular amusement in the mid-1800s. Each picture sequence, hand painted on the face of a wheel, represented a figure in action, such as this acrobat tumbling on a rope. Some disks had an additional design closer to the center so two actions could be viewed simultaneously. Phenakistoscopes like these and other optical toys are displayed at America Hurrah Antiques in New York.

D

Figure D: To make a movie wheel of a walking cat, as detailed on page 2932, trace this pattern, cut out the circle, and glue it to bristol board. Then cut out the wheel and the slits.

at a time and to see the next picture so quickly that the after image of the previous picture was still retained. Moreover, the lapse of time between images had to be equal. A quickly spinning wheel and even spacing of the pictures solved the problems. The first was handled by putting evenly spaced viewing slits around the edge of the disk. When the viewer spun the wheel, holding it in front of his eyes with the drawings facing a mirror, the slits kept each picture separate while the speed of the wheel and the even spacing of the images caused the eye to perceive a figure in motion rather than a series of still drawings. Thus was the motion picture born.

E
Figure E: Trace this pattern of a Martian, smiling as a rocket and star spin past him. Cut out the pattern, glue it to bristol board, and cut out the bristol-board wheel and the viewing slits.

Round and Round
To duplicate either of the picture wheels shown in Figures D (page 2931) and E (above), you will need: a pencil; masking tape; 8-by-10-inch sheets of tracing paper and 4-ply bristol board; scissors; rubber cement; colored felt-tipped markers; an upholstery tack; and an unsharpened pencil or 10-inch dowel.

Trace either pattern; then cut out the circle (do not cut the slits at this point). Trace this circle onto the bristol board and cut it out as well. Use white glue to secure the tracing, right side, to the bristol board. When the glue is dry, cut out the slits with a scissors or craft knife.

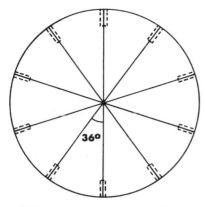

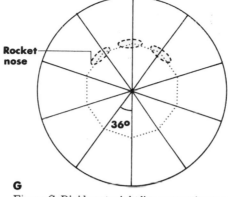

F

Figure F: To make a movie wheel, scribe a circle at least 7½ inches wide on bristol board. Using a protractor, divide the circumference of the circle into ten 36-degree segments. Then draw straight lines through the center of the circle to connect the points that lie opposite each other.

G

Figure G: Divide a straight line connecting two adjacent lines where they cut through the inner circle into a number of equal parts matching the number of pictures, in this case, nine. Using such dots as a guide, you can gradually advance successive images so all are spaced evenly.

Color the wheel, using the same colors in each frame of the series. To attach the wheel to the dowel, push an upholstery tack through the center of the wheel and into the dowel, ½ inch from one end.

To see the pictures move, stand in front of a mirror and hold the wheel in front of your eyes. Holding the handle, spin the wheel in the direction of movement indicated in the picture series. Keep both eyes open and peep through the viewing slits. The pictures reflected in the mirror will seem alive.

Designing Movie Wheels

To design your own movie wheel, draw ten pictures of one figure, each in a slightly different pose. Together the pictures should form a cycle of action that begins and ends in the same place. Let the first half build up to a climax in the action, with the second half returning gradually to the starting point.

When the cat shown in Figure D is revolved, he appears to walk. No two drawings are alike and the cycle could start anywhere, but only five basic drawings were needed, since the shading of the legs could be reversed in the second five. More typical is Figure E, in which the Martian face, when spun, will appear to burst with laughter because the expressions of his mouth, eyebrows, cheeks, and chin gradually change through half the frames from a smile to a laugh. The identical four pictures were repeated, in reverse, to complete the second half of the cycle, from the laugh back to the smile. Extreme movements such as the smile and laugh always are opposite on a picture wheel.

Another optical illusion you can introduce in making a movie wheel is also shown in Figure E. The outer circle (the Martian) has an even number of frames, ten. But the inner circle, the rocket, has an odd number of frames, nine. These images will appear to move around the circle backwards—that is, opposite to the direction of the spin.

To make a movie wheel, scribe a 6- to 8-inch circle on bristol board, and divide it into ten equal segments (Figure F). Cut viewing slits in the edge of the circle ⅞ inch deep, using Figure D or E as a guide. Draw your pictures on the wheel, spacing the pictures evenly.

To make the inner circle of action, scribe a circle 2 inches smaller than the wheel itself. Sketch a figure (such as the rocket) small enough to fit nine times around the new circle. All nine images must be spaced equally around the circle. To determine this spacing, draw a straight line connecting two adjacent spokes that intersect the circle (Figure G). Divide this length into nine equal parts. Mark the line with dots at these points. Duplicate these lines and dots around the inner circle. Position the first image touching a spoke, the second touching the first dot to the left of the next spoke, moving counterclockwise. Let each succeeding image overlap the line by one more dot. Paste or trace these images in place and they will be equally spaced. All should face in the same direction.

Paper Folding and Cutting
Zoetropes

The zoetrope, a revolving moving-picture drum, was invented in 1834 by Englishman William Horner. It was a cylinder with viewing slits near the top. A series of pictures on a paper strip lined the drum. To see the picture move, the viewer looked through the slits as the drum revolved beneath a light source. Since the top of the drum was open, zoetrope strips could be interchanged easily to show a variety of pictures. Many early zoetrope strips portrayed animals; so the toy was often called a zootrope.

Some of the original zoetrope drums were quite large and ornate. Lamplight was used to illuminate the picture strip, adding to the contrast between its white background and the dark color of the drum.

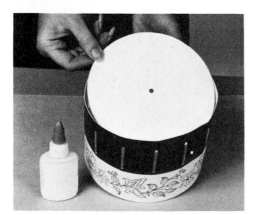

3: After you have glued the side rectangle into a cylinder, reinforce the joint by gluing the interfacing over the seamline. Press the three layers together until the glue dries.

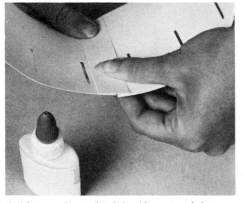

4: Brush glue inside the cylinder next to its bottom edge. Then press the 6-inch disk down into the cylinder until it rests flat at the bottom. Waxed paper beneath the assembly will keep the drum from sticking to the work table as the glue dries.

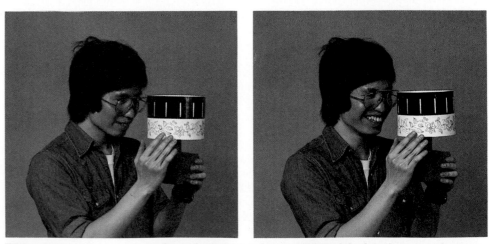

With a picture strip in a zoetrope drum, the device is held near a light and the drum is spun. A viewer looking through the slits sees pictures merge together into lifelike motion.

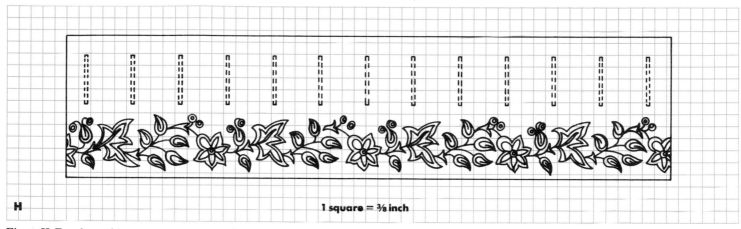

H

1 square = ⅜ inch

Figure H: To enlarge this pattern for a zoetrope drum, draw a grid of ⅜-inch squares on tracing paper and outline the viewing slits, copying one square at a time. You can enlarge the floral motif for the bottom half of the drum in the same way if you like.

A Different Drum

To make a zoetrope like the one shown opposite, you need: one 18-by-24-inch sheet of tracing paper; carbon paper; 4-ply bristol board; and black flint paper. (The flint paper is available at art supply stores). In addition you need: ruler; pencil; craft knife; scissors; compass; masking tape; awl; white glue; rubber cement; wax paper; and newspapers. For the stand you will need: a large wooden spool; a 2½-inch flatheaded wood screw; two fender washers; a drill and bit matched to fit the hole in the spool; a screwdriver; and a 4-by-4 block of wood about 3 inches high. Marking pens and paint can be used to decorate the drum.

Enlarging the Pattern

To begin, enlarge the pattern for the zoetrope drum slits (Figure H). Cut out the pattern and tape it to the bristol board. Using carbon paper, transfer the viewing slits to the bristol board. Remove the carbon and tracing.

Cut out the bristol-board rectangle but not the slits. Cut a 2 5/16-by-19-inch rectangle of black flint paper. Using rubber cement, glue the flint paper (right side up) to the unmarked side of the bristol board. Align the flint paper with the top edge of the bristol board. When the cement is dry, cut out each of the 13 slits with a craft knife, guided by a ruler. The black flint paper will be on the outside of the drum.

Decorating the Drum

You can decorate the lower half of the outside of the drum with the floral motif shown, coloring it as you wish. Or use gift wrap or wallpaper instead.

To turn the rectangle into a cylinder, cut a 1/2-by-4 7/16-inch piece of bristol board for an interfacing. With the decorated side of the drum face down, roll the ends gently toward the center until they meet. Overlap the ends by ¼ inch and glue them together; then glue the interfacing over the seam line (photograph 3).

Using a compass, scribe and cut out two circles of bristol board, one 6 inches and the other 6 1/16 inches in diameter. Use an awl to pierce a 3/8-inch hole in the center of each circle. Then cover your work table with wax paper. Brush white glue along the inside bottom edge of the cylinder, and stand it on the wax paper. Push the 6-inch disk into the cylinder until it lies flat at the bottom (photograph 4). Let the glue dry. Then turn the drum upside down. Glue the second disk to the bottom of the drum (photograph 5).

Making the Stand

To make the zoetrope stand, drill a hole ½ inch deep in the center of the wood block, using a bit the size of the spool hole. Glue the spool to the block so the holes line up. Paint the base and spool, and let dry. To assemble the zoetrope, put a washer on the screw and push the screw through the hole in the bottom of the drum. Put another washer on the screw; then turn the screw into the spool and wood block (photograph 6). Tighten the screw just enough so the drum is attached to the block but can spin freely.

5: Turn the drum upside down and glue the larger disk over the closed end.

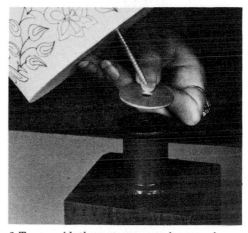

6: To assemble the zoetrope, put a large washer on a wood screw, and thread the screw through the hole in the drum bottom. Add another washer and drive the screw through the spool and into the wood block. Do not tighten it so much that the drum will not spin freely.

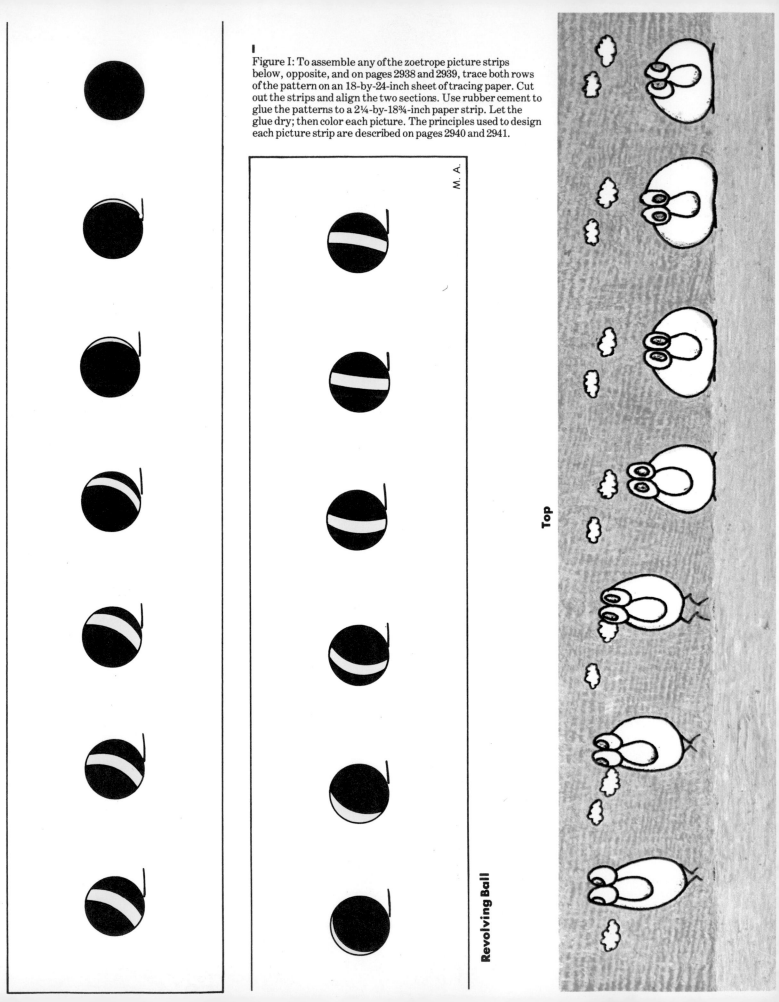

Top

Figure I: To assemble any of the zoetrope picture strips below, opposite, and on pages 2938 and 2939, trace both rows of the pattern on an 18-by-24-inch sheet of tracing paper. Cut out the strips and align the two sections. Use rubber cement to glue the patterns to a 2¼-by-18¾-inch paper strip. Let the glue dry; then color each picture. The principles used to design each picture strip are described on pages 2940 and 2941.

M. A.

Top

Revolving Ball

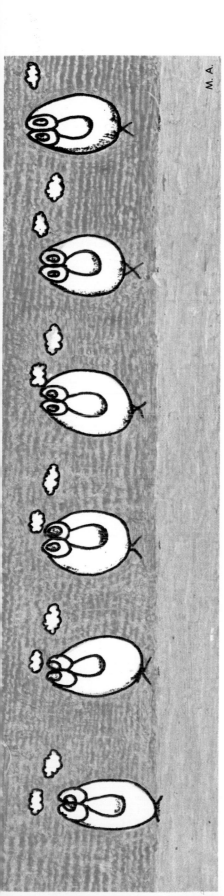

Bobbing Line Character

Top

Blackbird Fly By

2937

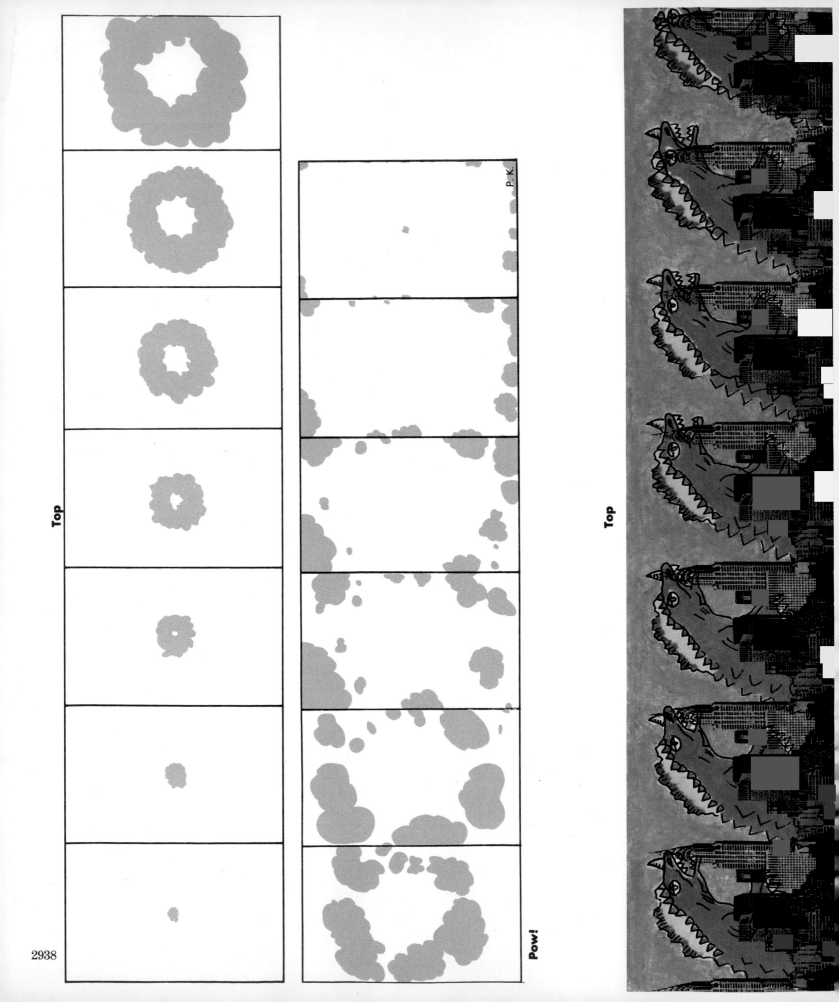

Top

Top

2938

Pow!

P.K.

Horror Movie

Top

Fun House

2939

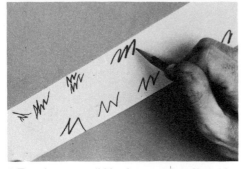

7: To animate a scribble, draw a series of jagged lines on a 2¼-by-18¾-inch paper strip. Put the strip in a zoetrope drum, and spin the drum to see the designs move.

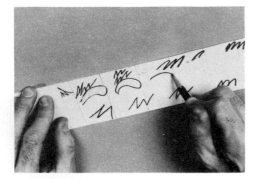

8: To draw a picture sequence on a paper strip, divide the strip into 13 frames, each 1 7/16 inches wide. Then draw the same worm design in the center of each box. Spin the strip in the drum and watch the worms appear to crawl.

Picture Strips

To make picture strips, you need a 2¼-inch-wide roll of adding machine tape or several 18-by-24-inch sheets of bond paper. Each strip should measure 2¼ by 18¾ inches. When the strip is placed in the drum, its ends should meet with the top edge just below the viewing slits.

To make a quick picture strip, scribble any design you like on one side of a paper strip (photograph 7). Place the strip inside the zoetrope and spin the drum. Although the designs were not drawn in sequence, they will appear to be in motion, joined in a continuous wave.

To heighten the illusion, divide the scribble strip into 13 boxes, each 1 7/16 inches wide. Repeat one image, such as a worm, in each box (photograph 8). Place the strip in the zoetrope and spin the drum. As the strip revolves, the worm will appear to squirm in a continuous movement.

One of the things that makes zoetropes such fun is the variety of images you can animate. The figures on pages 2936 through 2939 will give you an idea of the range possible. To use any of them, duplicate the patterns, following the instructions in Figure I; then put the picture strip in the drum and watch it come to life.

Revolving Ball

When spun in a zoetrope, the revolving ball shown in Figure I will appear to spin in place. The strip was divided into 13 equal boxes or frames, and a circle was centered in each, as shown in Figure J. The illusion of spinning is achieved with an arc drawn on the circle in 13 slightly different positions. In this way the circle becomes a striped ball. A dark line drawn on one side of the circle's bottom edge gives the ball weight and shadow. So that the ball's gradual change of position can be easily seen, the stripe is colored red. As the stripe gradually disappears, then reappears, it seems that the ball has completed one revolution. When the strip is in the zoetrope and spun, the ball repeats this rotation in a continuous cycle.

Bobbing Character

Just as a circle can become a ball, it can be stretched and squashed to represent a character (Figure I). But in this strip two new elements have been added. First, the character appears to bob up and down. Figure K shows how the character was placed in each frame to achieve this. Exaggerating the contrast between the stretch and squash positions creates an impression of body weight; varying the facial expressions gives personality. Shaded areas added to the body and below the feet create depth.

The second new element is the added clouds. Since 12 clouds are positioned over 13 viewing frames (pages 2936 and 2937), they appear to move from left to right as the character bounces up and down.

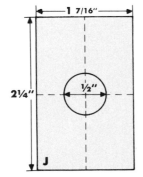

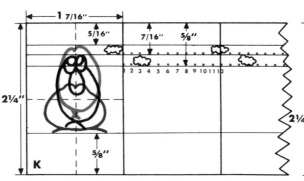

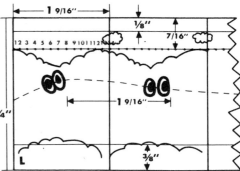

Figure J: The secret behind the revolving ball animation shown on page 2936 is that the circle representing the ball stays in the same place in each frame, while the arc drawn in it changes position. For plotting this, two guidelines were drawn in each box to divide it in half horizontally and vertically. Then a ½-inch-circle template was centered over the intersection of the guidelines and outlined on the paper.

Figure K: The character in the picture strip on pages 2936 and 2937 is horizontally centered in each frame, just as the revolving ball was (Figure J), but his vertical position changes. To plot his movement, two guidelines were ruled 5/16 inch from the top and ⅝ inch from the bottom edge of the strip. To plot the line the clouds should follow, two parallel guidelines were drawn, 7/16 and ⅝ inch from the top edge of the strip.

Figure L: To create the blackbird picture strip on page 2937, a treetop design was drawn on tracing paper and transferred to each box of the strip with carbon paper. A guideline at the top of the strip determines the path of the cloud. A wavy guideline, indicated by the dotted lines above, was drawn to create the up and down movement of the bird's flight, and a figure was drawn on this line every 1 9/16 inches.

Blackbird Fly By

Zoetrope designs can be plotted to move horizontally, as in the blackbird strip in Figure I. Whenever the number of images is one more or less than the number of viewing slits, the image will seem to move horizontally. In each of these 13 boxes, a treetop design is centered (Figure L). Then 14 clouds were evenly spaced within the strip, so they will seem to move from right to left. (Half a cloud was placed at the right and left edges of the picture strip to complete the cycle as they meet.)

Finally, 12 bird drawings were evenly spaced on a wavy path crossing the 13 boxes. Since the number of birds and boxes is not the same, the bird will also appear to move, but in the direction opposite to the clouds.

Pow!

Explosion effects, like that in Figure I, are often used in animated cartoons. They are easy to draw if you follow a symmetrical guide (Figure M). The trick in this design is to draw a box, which is the same size as one frame, on tracing paper. Then draw 13 circles, concentric to the center of the box (Figure M). This guide shows you how much of the circle will remain inside the box as it enlarges.

The explosion begins with a small circle resembling a puff of smoke. Gradually a concentric circle emerges and both circles grow to form a billowy smoke ring. Once the edge of the smoke ring collides with frame lines it appears to explode. Only fragments of the ring appear in subsequent frames. Finally, a small circle is centered in the last frame to signal that the explosion is ready to repeat.

Spooky Creatures

A miniature fun house or horror movie can be put in a zoetrope drum (Figure I). The principles used are similar to those used earlier and are shown in Figures N and O. The horror movie strip shows how useful a copying machine can be in making animations. For the city skyline to remain exactly the same from frame to frame, a section of a postcard was duplicated 13 times. The pictures were then pasted in the 13 boxes. The monster appears to pass through the city because he was drawn in only 12 positions.

In the fun house strip, the skeleton and spider appear in each of 13 boxes. The skeleton raises his arm and the spider descends as the drum revolves. But the bug at the bottom of the strip seems to move forward because he was drawn 14 times.

You can make a picture strip with photographs by pasting 13 small black-and-white photographs to a strip of paper. Here, Martin Abrahams demonstrates a picture sequence of one completed action by blowing up a balloon and then letting it deflate. In the first ten frames, the balloon expands. Then pictures Nos. two, four, and seven are repeated in reverse order to show the balloon getting smaller. The last picture in the sequence merges into the first to form a complete cycle.

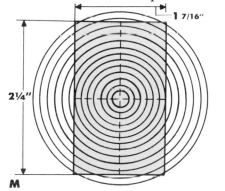

Figure M: To determine how to space the smoke in each frame of an animated explosion, a guide the same size as one frame is used. Starting at the center of the box, 13 concentric circles are scribed, one for each box. Working from the circle's center, use this guide to determine the amount of the explosion that appears in each frame as the picture sequence progresses. Fragments of smoke appear in the frames following the explosion.

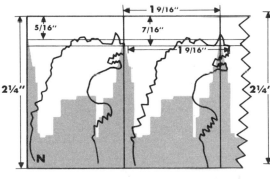

Figure N: To plan the horror-movie strip, a guideline was drawn 5/16 inch from the top edge of the strip to indicate where the tip of the highest building should fall. Similarly, a guideline was made 7/16 inch from the top edge of the strip to indicate where the tip of the monster's nose should be. Dots spaced 1 9/16 inches apart along this line were used to position the figure evenly around the picture strip.

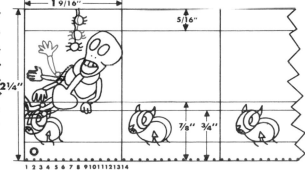

Figure O: For the spooky-creature strip, guidelines were drawn 5/16 inch from the top and 11/16 inch from the bottom to position the skeleton in each box. The spider moves on a vertical guideline centered in each box, and the bug images are aligned between two guidelines ¼ and ¾ inch from the bottom. The first image is placed on the frameline at the far right; the remainder is spaced to fall short of each successive frame.

9: A tracing pad is useful for making a flipbook. Start on the last page and draw the last image at the right of the page. Skip two pages and draw an image in the middle of a page. Skip two more pages and draw the image at the left of the page. Then fill in the positions that occur between those you have drawn.

10: You can add a second image to a flipbook. Both will move simultaneously if you place the second design near or over the first, again working from the back of the pad to its front.

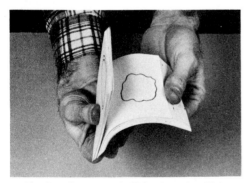

11: To view the pages of a flipbook made with index cards, first stack the cards in order of the picture sequence. If the book is to be flipped from the front, put the first card in the sequence on top. Bend the cards at the middle and slightly fan the edge to be flipped. Then release the cards, one at a time, from under your thumb.

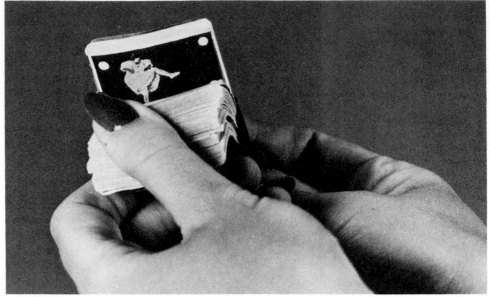

When the camera was first used to take pictures of figures in action, the pictures were often put into flipbook form. When the pictures were arranged in proper sequence and flipped quickly, the effect was that of animation.

Paper Folding and Cutting
The flipbook

The kineograph, a flipbook patented in 1868, is a small book with one picture of a sequence on each page. As the pages are flipped, the picture series will appear to move continuously.

To make a flipbook, you will need; a 9-by-12-inch tracing pad; an empty 3-by-5-inch note pad with at least seven pages, or seven 3-by-5-inch index cards; and an assortment of colored pencils or felt-tipped markers.

To get an idea of how these movie books work, staple seven 3-by-5-inch sheets of paper together. Make sketches that plot three main actions that approximate what happens at the beginning, middle, and end of the book. For example, turn to the last page of the pad and draw a wavy line in the lower righthand corner. Then every two pages, draw a similar line, moving it gradually from right to left (photograph 9). Starting at the beginning, evenly space wavy lines on the in-between blank pages. When you flip all seven pages, you will see the line appear to move. To make the animation more interesting, add another element, such as a circle, to the line. Again, start at the last page and plot the three extreme moves of the circle every two pages, shifting it from the bottom to the middle and then to the top of the line (photograph 10). Draw the in-between positions, flip the pages, and the line and the circle will seem to move.

Tracing paper is best for planning sequences, but to make a picture book to flip quickly, draw each picture on note paper or index cards. When you draw an image on an index card and hold it over a light source, then place blank cards over it, you can trace the image at various places to plot a path of action. To flip a stack of index cards, hold an end in each hand and bend the cards at the middle. Then flip one end of the stack with your thumb (photograph 11).

Story Books
If you like to draw, you can make a picture storybook, such as *How Clouds Came to Be*, shown opposite. Seven of the main actions are pictured; when all of the in-between positions are added, the flipbook will have 25 pages. It starts with the clown's profile at left and an arc in the background for a sun. By page six the clown has moved to the right and the sun has begun to rise. By page eight the clown has moved two steps to the right and is facing forward, and the sun's face is visible.

Shown above are illustrations from a 25-page story book, *How Clouds Came to Be*. To complete the story, draw the missing pictures that lie between these main actions, each on a separate index card. Then flip the cards quickly to animate the picture story.

Three pages later the clown's hand has moved to his head and the sun's face has a smile. On page 15 the clown's arm has moved down and he has removed a ball from his pocket. On page 17 the clown tosses the ball, angering the sun. On page 19 the clown puts his hands over his ears as the sun and ball collide and explode. Finally on page 25 the explosion disperses into clouds and the clown waves goodbye.

To make the storybook, trace the clown shown in profile in Figure P. Transfer that drawing to six cards, holding card and drawing against a windowpane. On each successive card, move the image a bit toward the right. Follow the same procedure with the rest of the cards, using the front view of the clown in Figure P. The drawing shows how the arm should be positioned on the various cards. Color the cards; then arrange them in order and flip them so the images seem to move in a lifelike way. To bind the cards as they are flipped, staple the free edges of the book opposite the clown image.

Figure P. To create the picture sequence for the flipbook, *How Clouds Came to Be*, copy these full-sized clown patterns on tracing paper, using a black felt-tipped marker. When you draw the clown use the arm gesture guide to make sure the arm is positioned correctly for the cards that come before and after it. To transfer a clown tracing, place it behind an index card and hold both up to the light while you trace the clown in different poses.

Some designs can be drawn that change completely as they are flipped. Here are three main actions from a ten-page flipbook in which a flower pot turns into a bird.

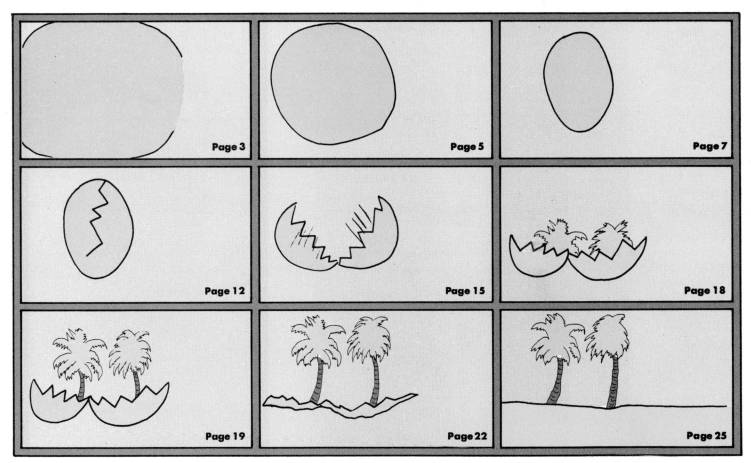

Nine main actions from a 25-page flipbook are given here. By adding the drawings between these, you can make a picture sequence in which a circle changes into two palm trees.

Fantasy Books

Flipbooks lend themselves to fantastic images that are transformed completely. Three extremes of a flower in a pot as it changes into a bird on a limb are shown above, top. Starting on the second page, the petals gradually change until they begin to resemble a bird (page five). Finally, the bird emerges (page ten). You will need to draw the positions that lie between these extremes on the index cards.

Nine pictures are shown below from a 25-page flipbook in which a circle changes into two palm trees. Starting with page three, a circle comes together and forms on page five. By page seven, the circle becomes an egg shape that cracks on page 12 and opens on page 15. Two trees rise from the shell on pages 18 and 19. From pages 22 to 25 the shell thins until it is only a horizontal line. Draw the in-between images to complete the picture sequence.

For related projects see "Cartoons," "Kaleidoscopes," and "Shadow Theater."